Legacy Publications

Pigs on the Patio

MY LIFE RIDING HERD ON A LOWCOUNTRY PLANTATION

By Liz Tucker

I would like to thank Legacy Publications,
especially Jane Iseley and David Bailey for having faith in me
and my writing. Their insight was invaluable.
I am also very grateful to my brother, Robert M. Smith, Jr.,
whose photographic company, PhotoVision in Columbia, South Carolina,
assisted in providing the photography for this book. His advice and
enthusiasm for the book were of great importance to me.

Editor / David Bailey
Design / Jaimey Easler
Copy Editor / Sarah Lindsay

Legacy Publications
1301 Carolina Street, Greensboro, NC 27401
www.pacecommunications.com/print/legacy.php
Printed in USA by RR Donnelley

It is my pleasure to dedicate this book to
Diji, Elizabeth, Richard and Courtenay . . . and The Saint . . .
who made this "slice of life" at Limerick so very special.

Contents

Photographs

Preface

Everyone remembers—surely they must—a certain time in his or her personal history that was more fun, more interesting, more exhilarating, more poignant, more hilarious, more filled with the very essence of life than any other time. I certainly do. For me, that most enthralling time occurred when my life, and the life of everyone in our entire family, revolved around Limerick Plantation. Located at the headwaters of the east branch of the Cooper River near Charleston in the very heart of the Lowcountry of South Carolina, Limerick became our house and home for an interlude that was sadly cut short.

This delectable slice of life bubbled with excitement and the exuberance of naive youth. Even though we were totally untutored in such matters and practically impecunious, my off-the-wall husband, our four children and I took up the challenge of plantation living, and took on the responsibility of nurturing and caring for an ever-changing assortment of animals, most of whom became our pets—whether they were coons or cows.

Actually, we had little or no choice when my husband's mother died unexpectedly. It was buy Limerick or lose it . . . forever. Since owning the plantation his family had acquired had been my husband's lifelong dream, ready or not, we were determined to find a way monetarily to make this happen. When all looked pretty hopeless, the father of one of our friends offered to co-sign a bank note, and soon Limerick became ours to have and to hold forever—or at least that's what we thought. We proceeded not only to hock our pocketbook but also to give up any semblance of the sophisticated, urbane Charlestonian lifestyle I had come to cherish. This was a decision that none of us will ever regret, but it set in motion a series of events that would be nothing short of life-altering. Although we were not sure of what we were doing, or how to do it, my husband and I were young enough and trusting enough to dive right in and go for it! Besides, if we had known what to do, we couldn't have afforded to do it. As a result, life at Limerick Plantation was just waiting for us to happen to it.

Limerick Plantation

Named in 1702 for Limerick, Ireland, historically it was
a rice plantation fifty miles northwest of Charleston in
South Carolina's "Lowcountry." The term is purely descriptive,
as the region is low, flat, sandy and watery. Along the coastline
from the Savannah River to just above Myrtle Beach, the
Lowcountry traces the ocean floors of prehistoric seas and stretches
inland to the prehistoric dunes (The Fall Line). But though
the Lowcountry is a geographic place, the definition goes
much deeper. It is a place of cultural singularity, and is referred
to as a paradise by most who live here.

Limerick's original 4,000 acres had been owned by
the Huger and Ball families in Colonial and antebellum days.
Our family was the first to live there full time since the Civil War,
but the remnant that we bought, which included the grand
avenue of oaks (the plantation house had long ago burnt to
the ground), was only 250 acres. Still, its old rice fields were ideal
for duck hunting, the river was prime for fishing, and its natural
woodland beauty made it a wonderful setting for the warm
memories and misadventures I'd like to share with you.
The house, set overlooking the old rice fields and nestled under
two enormous live oak trees, was relatively new, but in ancient
surroundings. I have come to think this a very proper way to live . . .
very much in today's world, yet always aware of, and fascinated
by, that which came before. Between those two enormous trees
lay The Patio, the heart of life at Limerick Plantation.

Cast of Characters

Mom | That's me, Liz. Native of Louisville, Kentucky.
Mother of four children, all of whom went to school fifty miles
away from Limerick. Therefore, I was not only the family chauffeur,
but also mower of grass, main cook and bottle washer, abettor in

daily adventures at Limerick and chief teaser of The Saint. Now a licensed guide in the city of Charleston, I am a continuing student of the Lowcountry of South Carolina—its history, mores and lifestyle.

Dad | Nick, alias "Saint Nick" or, as hereafter called, "The Saint." He was Liz's tutor in the ways of the Lowcountry and a man who defied precise characterization. He listened to a different drumbeat for sure, ruled the family with a firm grip, was a workaholic in his career and an extremist in all he did. His main interest above anything else was hunting, especially duck hunting, which is the real reason we were living at Limerick.

Diji | Older Son Diji, or Nick Jr., was pleasant and fun-loving, but anxious to become a teenager, and after he adopted the modish garb of the day, including very long hair, bell-bottom trousers and faded T-shirts, he became the number-one object of diatribes from The Saint. His love for The Grateful Dead at deadly decibels certainly didn't improve matters.

Elizabeth | Older Daughter, idolizer of her older brother, Elizabeth was also pretty, smart and sociable. She therefore found life at Limerick to be a trial since we lived so far away from her friends and the action in town.

Richard | Second Son Richard thrived on Nature's ways and loved living at Limerick. His drumbeat was one that echoed his father's, but was even more distant. In his inimitable way, Richard supplied much of the excitement and surprises that enlivened our plantation life.

Courtenay | Younger Daughter Courtenay took care of us all! The natural environment at Limerick and growing up with brothers and a zealot father reinforced her determination to be a tomboy, and she was rarely seen without her camouflage hunting hat. Her enthusiasm for everything and her organizational skills overwhelmed us all, and Dad was putty in her hands.

Never Let Your Raccoons Eat Bubble Gum

I **welcome you to Limerick** Plantation as it was on one particular day several decades ago. As I recall, I was desperately searching for—and honestly believed there should be—a reasonable, rational explanation for the last fifteen minutes of my life. I was a reasonable person, with a reasonable family, living a reasonable life. Or so I thought as I raced to extricate our two pet raccoons from a five-pound bag of flour that they had just detonated in the kitchen. I watched in exasperation as clouds of white biscuits-to-be hung in the air and our pet, Ricky Raccoon, beat a hasty retreat to the relative safety of the innards of our grand piano.

I was successful in catching the second raccoon (Ricky's sister), and I put her in time-out in the garbage compactor while I tried to figure the best way to tackle the awful mess. It was only yesterday that I had, quite happily, stumbled upon the idea of using the garbage compactor as a coon-storage spot while trying to remove these two little rascals from the refrigerator . . . they love bacon, you see. Warring with creatures that have four hands instead of two had made me very creative in outwitting them.

Closing them in the compactor with something they liked was just the ticket . . . no mess while they eat fried chicken, and I have five minutes of quiet—which is worth all the tea in China, when one is contemplating leading a reasonable, rational life!

In the midst of this floury white-out, my two younger children, Richard and Courtenay, raced inside with the triumphant news that they had succeeded in teaching Walter, the pigeon, to fly. Actually, I was pleased, since just last week they had failed so miserably with Franklin, the duck, who, being much too heavy to fly, had crashed into the fence, breaking his neck in the process. Not wanting to bring up this unpleasant thought, I congratulated Richard and went outside on The Patio to watch Walter sail gracefully overhead, waggle his wings, and disappear into the distance, probably forever (if he had any sense).

As I stood on The Patio, I surveyed my domain here at Limerick Plantation, located deep in the heart of the Lowcountry in what is known locally, and historically, as Hell Hole Swamp. Disregarding the ominous mental picture that name evokes, I looked out over the panorama that encompassed our home. It was a lovely, pastoral sight with its watery ponds, huge oak trees dripping with moss, and green pastures filled with cows. The quietude belied the chaos I was experiencing in the house. In the distance (nearly a mile away), the tallest trees grew along the banks of the Cooper River. That is the place we called The Point, our main access to the river and a favorite gathering spot for the family.

I would have preferred to linger on The Patio, absorbing all this beauty, but I was forced to return to reality when I noticed that our busy white rabbit had eaten the heads off all ninety-five marigold plants that had been planted earlier in the week. (This prodigious planting took place after a recent visit to Biltmore House in Asheville, where, à la Vanderbilt, I was introduced to the concept of more, which I was told makes a bigger splash.) Gripe! I turned to go back to my kitchen mess . . . a much bigger splash.

At this moment, in these most reasonable few minutes, one of the timber-cutting crew drove up to report that two of our cows were out on the highway again. Double gripe! I sent the two older children, Diji and Elizabeth, off with the timber man to fetch them back, while I went to get the vacuum cleaner.

As that most valued machine roared into action, I wondered whether others who reside on plantations have raccoons in their garbage compactor; whether I was the only one who kept house with mud-daubers' nests on the picture frames, with little green tree frogs in every nook and cranny, and fire ants in the baseboards; and whether other housekeepers are reconciled to the daily possibility of cohabitation with the local reptiles.

You haven't lived until you have discovered a sizable snake wrapped around the towel bar in your bathroom or, while vacuuming the living room, seen the tail of a sizable snake protruding from under the chest of drawers. The only good thing about this sight was that there were no rattles on its tail. While I was wondering what to do about this situation (shooting would surely leave holes in the wall), the vacuum took over and slurped up the snake in a jiffy! The snake never knew what hit him! Now what was I to do? There really was no choice. I hauled the vacuum out onto The Patio, opened it, and gingerly removed the bag, which was writhing menacingly. Desperately, and with finality, I heaved the bag, with snake, as far as I could throw it and went back to my regular household tasks. All in a day's work, n'est-ce pas?

Work prompted me to think of vacation, the last one we'd had, spending a week at the beach. Logistics for that trip were daunting. I remember we left Limerick with four children, two raccoons still on the bottle, a dog, two cats who despised each other, four gerbils and a giant bullfrog in a saucepan . . . the last to satisfy a request from a photographer who needed a frog for a commercial. The ultimate outcome of that auspicious holiday was that the cats ate the gerbils, the frog escaped a scalding drip in the bathtub by hopping into the toilet, which, in no uncertain terms, was off-putting to those who were not aware that this relocation had taken place. And then the coons stole Courtenay's bubble gum . . . and that was only the first day! The real lesson learned on that one day was: Never give your raccoons bubble gum, or you will truly regret it!

Pushing that thought aside, I went to let the raccoons out of the compactor and decided that perhaps we should all go fishing. Now, that was a reasonable idea.

My Charleston of Old

Before that chaotic day at Limerick just described, this saga
began for me over fifty years ago when my family moved to
the Lowcountry of South Carolina from Kentucky.
This was a happening of immense significance for all of us in my
family. After all, our people had been in Kentucky since the earliest
days of that state's existence. My parents just picked us up, lock,
stock, and barrel, as the saying goes, and moved us all to Charleston.

As a rising senior in high school, I thought this move to be
truly catastrophic, but the move was accomplished, dropping
my brother, my sister and me into the heart of ancient and
fascinating Charleston. By coming to Charleston when we did,
in the early 1950s, my father, who was in the advertising business,
soon discovered that Charleston was twenty-five years behind the
business world he had left behind. (He always jokingly said that we
had emigrated!) But my mother loved the subtropical flowers and
the quiet grace of Southern hospitality in her new home. In this
Old Charleston, everyone knew everyone else—or about everyone.

Local terminology put me definitely in my place: I was, without doubt, a Cum Ya (the Gullah term for newcomer) to Charleston. Although I had been content with my Bin Ya status (been here forever) in Kentucky, the appeal of the new was inescapable, and I embarked on becoming a very zealous Cum Ya—and I still am.

Although I had been raised in the South, the lifestyle in Charleston was quite different. For one thing, they ate rice—copious quantities of rice. (In Kentucky, the standard fare had been potatoes, with rice reserved for Sunday dinners.) Charleston fathers left their offices to walk home for midday dinner, prepared by servants who had been with the families for generations. These men did not return to work until after enjoying a very civilized nap. Families moved to the beaches and/or to the mountains for the summers as they had for generations. People endured palmetto bugs (huge cockroaches) with grace! In fact, life was lived graciously, even though quite often one might observe a table in a beach house kitchen or dining room with its legs resting in four bowls of water to keep the ants away! At such a table, I had my first taste of okra soup, served by one of the revered Grand Dames of Old Charleston from a beautiful china tureen. I don't know which was the more awesome: okra or the grandmother!

In those days, there were children everywhere, gathering each afternoon at the East Bay Playground, the town's answer to not having large yards in which to play. There were greengrocers' shops on many a corner, where the ground floor of a once-noble townhouse had been usurped for commercial purposes as the city slipped into its own past. Unpainted and often covered with vines, many other grand homes had been split into efficiency apartments to house the hordes of naval personnel who were here during the war. Warehouses on the Cooper River still housed goods for shipping and were located practically next door to some of the most beautiful gardens in the city. The pace was slower, and the sleepy, well-mannered grande dame called Charleston just stole my heart.

The comparison my father made of Charleston to a Sleeping Beauty was entirely fitting. I am very glad that I can say I was here before she was completely awake: before the prosperity so visible now in Charleston, Beaufort, Georgetown and Savannah; before the vines were off the walls and when tourism was still very seasonal; before the wide thoroughfares and new bridges were built; before the tree-lined country roads leading to old plantations and country houses were widened and filled with commercial suburbia; and before Charleston was discovered anew.

I found this Lowcountry to be a place so beautiful, so interesting and so pleasant that in a matter of days, no matter what the initial thoughts may have been about being uprooted from Kentucky, the charm of the Lowcountry worked its magic on each of us in my family. And the love for this incredible region has grown with the years.

Thus, the seedling was planted. I knew the transplanting process had begun wholeheartedly when I received my first wedding present—a rice steamer. And then my mother-in-law taught me how to cook grits! My education had begun in earnest indeed.

Now, as I look back, I can see that Fate also played a role in my future life. By chance, on the second day after my arrival in South Carolina, I was introduced to the very fellow who would eventually become my husband. My own fate was sealed with that introduction, and the results have provided most of the material for the discourse that follows.

The New Pond

From the very beginning, the man who was to become my husband—the father of my four children, helpmate, benefactor, mentor, tutor in the ways of the Lowcountry, and above all, a challenge to any semblance of a reasonable life— showed the traits of an individualist beyond measure. Besides the fact that he was really cute, this is what appealed to me the most about him. He would never have been labeled, to use the argot of the era, a nonconformist, but his determination to challenge conventional thinking was as natural to him as it was for Richard to adopt orphan birds, hoping to teach them to fly. He just couldn't help himself. He thought about things in ways unimaginable to the average person. It was as simple as that—a quirk of the brain. Since I come from a long line of independent thinkers (my parents were referred to as "arty"), I should have recognized clues that hinted that it would be our lot in life never to be like other people. That notwithstanding, we seemed to make a good pair as we headed off into the sunset from the altar of St. Michael's.

I have already dubbed my husband St. Nick. In time, he gained a variety of nicknames according to what suited the occasion and to which he always responded happily, undeterred by any hints of lurking sarcasm. I will have to admit that teasing The Saint became one of life's great pleasures. As you'll see, he gave me plenty of opportunities, but few that compared with his determination to construct a new pond in the front of our house at Limerick.

As one approaches Limerick from State Highway 402, which was once part of the 18th-century King's Highway, the drive passes through an ancient avenue of live oak trees, which once led to the original plantation house. In our day, the drive continued beyond the avenue of oaks and old house site, making a circular drive in front of our house. Ninety percent of the year, this circle remained boggy and wet, rarely drying out, and The Saint had always envisioned a lake there, at least one that was more than ankle deep. Since life is made from dreams, I was in agreement— or so I thought. (I should explain that this was the actual front of the house, though most people referred to the patio side, which overlooks the rice fields, as the front.)

I remember one Saturday when Old Dreamer invited me up on the roof to discuss this idea of his. Who could refuse such an invitation? Certainly not I, so we made our way to the lofty rafters high above The Patio. Standing next to the chimney, he, with great sweeps of his arms, described what he had in mind. He didn't want just any old pond. No indeed. It must be a scenic pond. This meant it could not be round. That was boring. Leaving out my own ideas that included an arched bridge to the island and perhaps a gazebo in which one could contemplate deep thoughts, I suggested he might like to have an island in the new pond, perhaps with a weeping willow tree on it. But, on general principle, he didn't seem to think that was a good idea. His mind was contemplating deep thoughts—how to make Limerick even more of a hunting paradise.

Moving right along, then and there, we drew up a plan for the pond on paper—the first step—a giant step?

As we sat there on the roof, I felt a kindred spirit with the birds that flew overhead and wished that I, too, could live my all my life with a bird's-eye view of this land that was so beautiful. With sketchbook in hand, we made our way down, cautiously, since the stepladder was precariously balanced on top of the doghouse. St. Nick was full of enthusiasm for this new project, which was, at that point, just an idea on paper.

Deep in the back of my mind lurked a memory of a pond that my father had dreamed about on our place in Kentucky. I am sure his was a dream not unlike The Saint's, but, if my memory serves me correctly, that Kentucky pond, once dug, never, I say never, held water. I mentioned this to The Saint, and his answer was typically confident and typically mistrustful of anything that was done in Kentucky. "Well, I won't have it dug, I will dig it myself." Now we were getting down to the nitty-gritty. Tractor work is manly, but digging with a shovel was definitely not in The Saint's work vocabulary. I mentioned this.

"Who said anything about a shovel? John is lending me his bulldozer."

"Oh," was all I could muster, knowing full well, or so I thought, that The Saint knew very little about bulldozers. I mentioned this as well.

"Now, don't worry about that. John is lending me his driver, too."

Again, I said, "Oh." But the conversation was over, The Saint having disappeared to watch the ballgame. That night at supper, Diji asked why we had been on the roof—a reasonable question, in the total scheme of things.

"We are going to build a new pond," I answered.

"On the roof?" he asked.

"No, silly," I countered. "Out front."

"We already have four ponds out front," Courtenay interjected.

"That's out back," we all said in unison. The next question was not so dumb.

"Where are you going to get the water for the pond, Dad?" asked practical Elizabeth. We all wanted to hear the answer to this question.

"Why, we will dig a well that will supply both the new pond and the cattle corral," was the ready answer. This was the first mention of a well. "I haven't talked to the well-digger yet, but, you know, we will probably hit underground springs, too," he added with a hint of anxious hopefulness.

Aha! At that moment I had the first suspicion of what was to come. Inevitably, there was going to be a new pond, but I had my doubts about a water well.

Still remembering the mudhole in Kentucky, I said in my most forceful manner, "Old Master . . . no well, no pond!" He readily acquiesced, and dinner resumed with flurried conversations about the new pond. Elizabeth hoped it would make a better swimming pool than the alligator-and-snake-ridden fishpond. Courtenay was going to stock it with fish. Richard began planning for a new flock of ducks. Diji and I crossed our fingers.

One day, I returned home to find a bulldozer parked outside the front door. It was a huge machine, parked there like the family sedan. I apologized silently for all I had thought the preceding day and wondered when the driver would come. I then noticed the note tied to the steering column of the bulldozer. It read, "If you can't get it started, please call this number . . ." The truth will out!

St. Nick was gleeful when he got home, but he could not get it started and was forced to call the number. In a short time, the man came, surveyed the projected pond site and gave his opinion that the pond could be dug in about a week, and he would be glad to do it—for a fee. Hooray! Hooray! I still did not have a well, but at least I wouldn't be a bulldozer widow. And (always the eternal optimist), who knew, maybe we would hit an underground spring!

The plow was on the tractor, and the two men wanted me to plow out an outline for my scenic pond. I found it much easier to express this on paper, so The Saint helped me out. The pond was begun that very minute.

Sheldon was the driver's name, and he came faithfully, every afternoon after work. For two weeks, he came every day—and then for a third. This boggy piece of acreage was not soft mud, as had been supposed, but the hard, indigenous clay of our region's subsoil, known as marl. When exposed to the air, marl is like cement! We would have a veritable swimming pool! Elizabeth was ecstatic.

In the meantime, on the sly, The Earl of Limerick took to the woods in the bulldozer, and at that point, I nearly did become a bulldozer widow. Wanting to study more on his wood duck pond plan, he steamed into the woods in his usual tractor-driving fashion, lurched over a hummock at full tilt, and nearly turned over. He was bruised and sore for a week, but completely undeterred.

As the weeks lengthened into a month of digging and our funds grew short, Old Digger took over the digging of the pond himself. Soon he was rather proficient in handling the bulldozer, and my worries eased a bit.

It was an interesting and rather unusual fact that during these long weeks of digging, there had been nary a drop of rainfall. For once, the weather was with us. Had it rained, digging would have been virtually impossible. Instead, Old Digger would mount his behemoth machine, turn on its lights, and work until eleven o'clock at night . . . every night. He seemingly loved every minute of it. However, the schedule of one week's digging was but a vague memory as time marched on. The pond had progressed considerably by this time, but I must interject that not only were we gifted with one island, but soon two islands appeared sculpturally from the murky deep! I was told that they were to make good nesting places for Richard's ducks, but everyone knew that an island represented that which did not have to be dug! I vowed to put a weeping willow tree on one of those islands.

By now, there were two concerns to be reckoned with. One was the fact that we were not yet finished and it was bound to rain. The other was that the bulldozer broke! There were still great piles of red earth on the far side of the pond, and there was a great gaping hole, broken by the two sculptural islands, in my front yard. There was never a sign of an underground spring. Nor was there a well. And, worst of all, no water. We began to refer to the new pond as our scenic mudhole! We weren't the only ones. Poor Saint! The boys at The Club were teasing him as well. He was very frustrated and, I imagine, a bit embarrassed. This went on for some time, and we all were careful in how we talked about our scenic mudhole, for we were quite aware of The Saint's tender feelings on the subject.

One day, I knew he was really desperate when I discovered our half-inch garden hose snaking, oh, so furtively, from the faucet outside the house into the pond, sending its tiny trickle of Eau de Hell Hole into that yawning abyss of red clay. Oh, what a man will do to preserve his ego! We knew better than to comment!

But then it rained. My, how it rained! Whatever had been held back all those months now came down with a vengeance, and the pond came close to running over! Dared we mention the phrase "his cup runneth over"? Definitely not. None of us had the courage to broach the subject of flooding. This was definitely the better part of valor.

One damp morning, I drove up to the house with my part-time housekeeper, Eliza Ravanel, who lived down the road in Hell

Hole Swamp. She had been witness all summer to the entire pond-building process, but she had never said very much about it. As she got out of the car she could not help noticing that the scenic mudhole was now completely full of water. Rolling her eyes heavenward, she summed up the situation in her pure Gullah dialect: "Do Jesus, Miz Tuckah, de tide done cum in!" It certainly had.

The new pond did not overflow. In fact, it has never again been without water. The ducks loved the islands, and the cows loved the shrubbery we planted on the scenic mud piles left when the bulldozer broke before completion. I was given a weeping willow tree for Christmas, and it was duly planted on the south island. And—something none of us had considered—this new pond became a prime frog-gigging spot for those so inclined. Country living was now at its best!

Whenever I am asked how, or why, we dug a new pond, when we already had so much water here, I have a ready answer: If one has a bulldozer, then one must really do something with it. In other words, "Where there's a will, there is a way."

I might add a word to the wise from one who knows: If anyone offers your husband a bulldozer, remember to "just say no"!

Richard's New Surprise

When Richard was nine or ten, he wanted a horse in the worst way. We still lived in the city and it certainly seemed unrealistic for us to have such an animal at that time, especially since none of us knew a thing about horses, including how to ride. The fact that the barn had been inadvertently burned at Limerick put the final quietus on the subject. However, with an eye to the future, Richard was given riding lessons for his birthday. In fact, a rather sizable sum was paid out for Richard to learn to lead a horse around the ring! He became very good at leading, but staying on the horse was another thing altogether. It did not appear that his talents dictated an equestrian future.

However, we made the move to Limerick that summer and our Richard's appeals for a horse (shades of *Richard III*) soared to new heights. All previous reasons for turning down such pleas were still in effect, plus some, so little attention was given to having horses in our lives. A mistake. Richard was a determined little boy.

Shortly after our move to the country, I was making the twenty-five-mile jaunt to the grocery store when I passed a friend who lived on a neighboring place, who hailed me and asked me to get some horse feed while I was in town. This I did, glad that I could be of help. When I returned home, I realized that I had been had! Unbeknownst to anyone, Richard and this neighbor were in cahoots. Richard had traded his own cow and calf for the neighbor's pony and colt! Pony, colt and friend were now standing in the front yard— no, let me amend that: They were standing on The Patio, right outside the living room. Our friend was grinning from ear to ear with mischievous delight, while I was struck dumb. Needless to say, Richard was elated as he led the pony around the yard, the baby colt following worriedly alongside. Only a little taller than our dog, the colt was just about the cutest animal on record. The mother pony was no raving beauty, however, and her name was Moonlight. Richard named the colt Daisy-Mae, and the pair came to be permanent fixtures in our lives that year. Well, what else could we do?

As aforementioned, there were no fenced fields and we had no real barn at Limerick, so Moonlight and Daisy-Mae took up residence in the front yard. Within a few days, it was apparent that Moonlight would have nothing whatsoever to do with a saddle, and it was not even two minutes before she picked up on our lack of horse sense. Of this, she took full advantage. Poor Richard. He gave up the idea of a saddle in favor of bareback, but Moonlight would only go in one direction: to the house. So, for endless hours, Richard would lead her away, as far as he could (we had paid good money for him to learn to do this); then he would hop on and ride back to the yard. "Good old Moonlight," he would say proudly, "Look, Mom. She brought me right back to the house," as though that was exactly where he wanted to go! Back and forth they went, little Daisy-Mae following anxiously all the time. Except for me,

Daisy-Mae and Moonlight, everyone was just as happy as could be.

I never had a fondness in my heart for Moonlight, but Daisy-Mae was another thing altogether. She looked like a toy hobbyhorse, and she grew cuter every day. Like all baby things, she was extremely curious and playful and constantly getting into things that were off-limits to horses. As summer lengthened into fall, we thought nothing of sharing our patio with these two ponies.

In fact, we became rather used to having the ponies on The Patio with us, especially since they seemed to be patio-broken. We found it unusual to have a pony be so "friendly." We enjoyed having our coffee on The Patio each morning, but it was not long before it was apparent that Moonlight liked coffee too, so we would save the last swallows for her. (We just said we saved the last swallows. Actually, she took them from us and never even paused to say thank-you.)

If Moonlight was hungry, she just walked up to the sliding glass door, put her nose against it and stomped her foot. She knew we would hurry with some food because we weren't sure what she would do if we didn't hurry!

Moonlight also made it clear she did not like to share her patio–dining room with any other critters. These ponies were barely tolerated by the dogs and vice versa. Answering the dog's pitiful yelp at the door one night, I found Rip, our wonderful, very mature golden retriever, wide-eyed, looking over his shoulder, his bowl of food in his mouth, and the pony in furious pursuit. What a sight! Rip was not going to share his dinner with that creature! In retrospect, Moonlight really was a pushy horse! But Richard loved her, and we loved to watch Daisy-Mae, so life, with horse, continued.

There was one particular morning that I shall never remember without suffering a slight case of the shivers. It was just after The Saint had left for work when we saw that Daisy-Mae, in her coltish curiosity, had eaten the plastic worm at the end of a fishing pole and the hook was now caught in her lip. Needless to say, this caused her to be quite frantic, and she was galloping round and round the yard with the fishing pole bobbing and bouncing along beside her. It must have been painful, and she was frightened to death. I know I was. Appalled at this sight, I leaped in the car, trying to catch Old Workaholic, only to find my tire was completely flat. I needed that Old Saint! Triple gripe! Now I was stuck with being the problem-solver. I did not relish this thought, because I had not a clue as to what to do. Since we had only been in the country a couple of weeks, I had not the foresight to see that, most probably, this situation was just par for the course—at the time, I thought this was way beyond what should be expected of me. Be that as it may, for the sake of Daisy Mae's safety and my sanity, I knew I had to get my brain in gear and cope!

It was a given that we must cut the barb and pull it on through if we were to help free Daisy Mae of the fishhook. The ensuing project seemed endless as the morning unfolded.

With the help of all the children (my four had been augmented by the five who lived across the road), we finally succeeded in catching Daisy Mae, who did not want to be caught, nor did Moonlight want us to catch her. But catch her we did, and wrestled her to the ground. (Yee-ha!) The cheering section was boisterous in its enthusiasm.

Now, here must be explained a basic fact about this family. Whenever something is needed, it simply is never where it is supposed to be—ever! I had sent for some pliers, but because of the family failing outlined above, the search for them took some bit of time, leaving me astraddle the unhappy pony for what seemed an eternity. I eventually had to settle for some fence cutters, which were a couple of feet long. I don't believe anyone, in his wildest imagination, could understand the difficulty I faced. Sitting atop a thrashing colt with a mad mother pony trying to get me away,

I was trying to tackle a half-inch fishhook with a two-foot set of fence cutters.

This was an endurance contest on both sides, but eventually we both won. The two ponies scampered away. I was exhausted, and must have looked funny too, because all nine children were laughing uncontrollably. Such indignities a lady must face when she lives in the woods! Now, I had only to tackle the flat tire!

As time went on, we became one big happy family. If we ate lunch on The Patio, so did the ponies. If I planted flowers, they came too, and unplanted them. If they were hungry . . . well, you already know that scenario. The rides on Moonlight became fewer, and the saddle was a complete no-no by now. Oh yes, we were one big happy family!

With school starting, there was not as much time to spend with the ponies, so they were left to amuse themselves a great deal more than before. It was not long before the ponies were much more proficient at cow-chasing than I was. However, their boredom reached a zenith one Tuesday, which was our late day in the city.

On that day, after successfully collecting all the children in town, always something of a miracle, I drove home to Limerick and down the avenue, arriving shortly after Old Saint, who was now standing on the front steps to greet us. This in itself was an unusual occurrence. He never stood on the porch to greet us! The look on his face was very peculiar also.

All was explained when we stepped inside the living room. Oh, my! A quick survey showed that both horses had quite obviously spent the day inside the house! Disorder reigned. One chair was overturned, and the rest were askew. I don't know why horses must blow on everything, but paper napkins were strewn everywhere, as were ashes from the ashtrays and the fireplace. And they had also enjoyed quite a feast. When all was tallied, they had eaten twenty pounds of scratch feed, fifteen pounds of dog food, most of a bag of horse feed and a half-bushel of pears. And the baby had eaten three straw baskets and the broom! *"Ma foi!"* my old French teacher would have said. The Saint said something quite unsaintly.

All I could think to say was that I was certainly glad they seemed to be housebroken as well as patio-broken.

Agricola, Agricolae

When we decided to assume the role of planters on
our plantation, we certainly felt that our lack of farm
knowledge should not stand in the way of such an
operation as we planned for Limerick. We reasoned that, surely,
anyone who could read, and who had eyes with which to observe
and ears to hear, should be able to put into practice the simple tasks
involved in agricultural pursuits. As far as equipment went, we had
a fine, if somewhat aged, Ford tractor, with a few attachments,
plus an ancient truck, which was soon to be defunct.

There was not enough high land to farm commercially. Then
again, all we wanted to do was grow some crops that migrating
ducks might like, have a vegetable garden from which we could
eat, and plant some soybeans and corn for the cows to eat. This
was very small-scale in the present world's realm of enormous
mechanized truck farms, but it was very large-scale for an
impecunious Saint, his wife and four children. Lack of equipment
could be a problem, but we felt that ingenuity and some rose-

colored glasses could overcome much. Our farming efforts, therefore, were necessarily unorthodox, and, at least fifty percent of the time, they were unsuccessful.

When we lived in the suburbs of Atlanta, we had dabbled in gardening of a sort and had loved every minute of it. The Saint, always a city boy, found himself fascinated with a bit of toil in the soil. In our Atlanta days we were renting a house that had a rather roomy back yard, much of it taken up with an old garage that leaned so far to the left that only the weight of the roof kept it upright. One day, in an unprecedented fit of home-project energy, The Saint and Diji took a baseball bat and literally knocked it flat. Once it was cleared, we had quite a plot of land available for planting our victory garden. It was a family project, though much of it lay in my lap since Old Dad was away during most of the week. All in all, it was a reasonable success (hence the name "victory garden"), but what I remember about it the most was the soil preparation. Of course, this was way before the days of our having any such thing as a tractor, and I am not sure that rototillers had been invented yet, so how to plow up this garden presented a problem.

Through the local grapevine I was given the name of someone who would come plow our little plot, and I made the arrangements. No one could have been more surprised to see a man at my back door who was attached to Lois the Mule! A mule in the middle of this big city! I wasn't expecting a mule, but Lois knew exactly what to do, and before long the earth was nicely turned, though periodically Lois would stop to roll over and wallow in the nice cool earth. Then the neighborhood would resound with the cries of "Git up dere, mule, git up!" accompanied by a few kicks and "gees" and "haws." Only when ready would Lois regain her upright position and finish the job. As far as I was concerned, the job was well done and we could get to the job of planting a vegetable garden. Lois the

Mule came to our aid for two years in succession, and we then lost track of her. So you see, we did have some gardening experience.

The first garden I remember at Limerick belonged to my mother-in-law. It was planted within chain-link fencing at the foot of the yard where she directed Limerick's handyman, Amos, to plant a vegetable garden. From this little patch she brought us wonderful gifts of fresh vegetables, and she was very proud of her endeavors. She was very proprietary over this garden and loved to refer to *her* tomatoes, *her* squash and *her* butter beans. In fairness, she did turn on the sprinkler when it was time to water the garden, but other than that, all the labor came from Amos. However, her labors were fruitful, and it was a garden of which to be proud. We were grateful for Amos!

Several years later, in my reign as the mistress of Limerick, we had no handyman, and since Amos had died and his co-workers had seen his ghost haunting the avenue of oaks at Limerick, it was most probable Limerick would never have a hired hand again. The underground pipes in the old garden were ruined, and in fact there was no longer a source of water down there at all. Any efforts toward agriculture had to be redesigned, or rather redefined. It was about this time that I began to glean the true meaning of a working plantation.

But, of course, I was thinking small, while Old Farmer in the Dell was thinking in terms of magnitude: fifty acres of corn here, sixty acres of soybeans there and a field of rye over yonder, not to mention a dove field planted with dove goodies. This involved great thought and planning on his part, a larger bill at the seed store, and the total involvement of all of us for a considerable length of time.

It was not long before I learned that one of the most important steps in achieving agriculture was in the procurement of large quantities of fertilizer—filthy stuff, to be sure. This became one of my prime duties. Day after day, I was sent in my trusty blue station wagon to the store to pick up a hundred pounds of this and twenty-five bags of that. As at the grocery store (where I spent the rest of my time), the feed and seed vendors were most happy to load the purchases into my car but were noticeably absent on the other end. I don't know where I got the idea that it was also my duty to hoist these things into the shed—maybe it was necessary to make room in the car for the children—but hoist I did.

In any case, Old Farmer became a man of the soil, and the boys and I developed considerable arm power. My station wagon developed a permanent sag to its hindquarters, and sported a fine crop of rye grass in the way-back. My curiosity over the need for such quantities of fertilizer brought forth a logical explanation. With every seed planted, a plop of fertilizer went with it, thereby giving the seed a jump on the weeds. A beautiful theory, which seemed to work in every field we passed on the highway, but it had the opposite effect for us. Our weeds seemed to thrive on fertilizer, and within a very short time would completely overwhelm our various crops. Bummer. Then the ugliest word in farming vocabulary came forth: the hoe. I especially did not relish being the hoer! So we put the ancient cultivator to work. This hooked to the tractor in such a way that by driving between the rows, the weeds were neatly removed and wonderful brown earth was thrown upon the roots of the favored plants. This worked beautifully if the rows were spaced correctly. Invariably, to cultivate one of our rows, we had to mash another with the wheels of the tractor. This, surely, was one of the clearest manifestations of trial and error, the process which seemed to rule our farming experiments.

Besides the cultivator, we had several other interesting pieces of equipment that, when attached to the tractor, managed to compensate for the lack of field hands. I marveled at all of this machinery, and learned a whole new vocabulary as I helped Old Mechanic attach them to the tractor. During such operations, there always seemed to be a need for a five-pound wrench, a strong boot with which to kick, and the exact number of great big cotter pins to ensure the equipment would stay with the tractor. There was something else called a drawbar, over which I learned a few words of my own! (More about that later.) The wrench was always missing, the boot always missed and permanently injured the shin, and there was always one less pin than was necessary. That this was always the case was a mystery, because those important things were always put back in their proper places. Always!

When, in fact, the disk or harrow or planter was affixed properly to the tractor, the true nature of Old Farmer in the Dell came to the fore. He was obsessed by that machine! No one but The Saint was allowed to drive this tractor. When he was aboard, it was full speed ahead. Why he was not propelled clear to heaven when he hit a rough spot is anyone's guess. I remember once, when watching from afar, we saw him go in the opposite direction from heaven as the tractor and plow accidentally went into the pond. Down, down, down, he went, the tractor right behind him. We breathed a huge sigh of relief when he surfaced some distance away, unscathed. Of course, the tractor stayed under. One child suggested that he might have been trolling for fish! He did not think this was funny. I wouldn't want to go so far as to suggest that he was reckless behind the wheel, just exuberant.

There was a time when there was a plan to plant lots of soybeans as fodder for the cows. This was one of the times when resourcefulness raised its elegant head. There were not enough of us to do the job efficiently, so The Saint hired a number of the children's friends to help. (Child labor, anyone?) He trained Courtenay, age ten, to drive the truck at five miles per hour. He then stationed two children on the hood of the truck and two on each side of the back of the truck to sow the seeds. They were instructed that it was necessary to broadcast the seed very broadly.

As the truck moved slowly around the field, two more were assigned the tailgate, throwing out some sort of dust that kept something bad from happening. The Saint stood in the middle of them all, directing like a symphony conductor and sounding the cadence for sowing. All hands were paid a pittance, with the promise of a bonus if the crop grew. They worked hard and seemed to think it quite an exciting adventure. It was only later that I learned the dust was a poison! (Child labor at its worst!) But this time the crops grew well and, thank goodness, so did the children!

Alas, the crop grew well until the cows discovered the field. They then ate the crop before we could give it to them, as was their usual way of doing things. "If at first you don't succeed . . ." became the new motto of Limerick during these agricultural days, especially when we were trying to grow corn.

Our antiquated planter deposited one seed at a time, with a dollop of fertilizer, and covered up the corn seed as it moved down the row. It was required of one of us to walk behind the planter to see that the seed came out as promised. In these days, Old Farmer was always the driver, thus escaping that hot, dusty, 150-mile walk. I was usually the walker!

But then there was the year when The Saint fractured two vertebrae and found himself in a back brace, unable (meaning not allowed) to drive his beloved tractor—right at planting time. I hid my amusement in the face of his misery, but I, too, loved to drive the tractor, and perhaps it was timely that for a change, he now had to walk behind—so very erect in his back brace!

Poor man. Old Farmer would come home from work, change his clothes and charge out the door with the invitation, "Come on, let's go watch the corn grow!" We tried harder and lost more of that crop than all the other farmers in South Carolina combined, never finding a solution to crop failure! Either corn was definitely our adversary, or else it was through our attempts at growing this crop that our real black thumb prevailed. Something foiled the crop every year, sometimes two or three times. One year, we planted corn seven different times! Although the seed was treated with a poison that was noxious to crows, these black pirates knew just where to go at just the right time to pull up the new green shoots and eat the seed kernels. If we were lucky enough to escape the birds, then the crop became dinner for the raccoons. They also liked corn. Even having appropriate fencing never hampered the progress of our cows if that was where they wished to be. But, should any corn survive a bovine attack or bird invasion and ripen to fullness, the raccoons moved back in with their magic fingers, climbed the stalks, peeled the shucks and dined happily. Amazingly, they put the shucks neatly back into place when finished so we could not see the damage done!

One year, the corn crop was first drowned by eleven inches of rain and then burned up by a severe draught. Not only did this dampen any agrarian spirit we gamely held, but it was definitely enough to obliterate any hope of cornstalks in the duck fields, which all duck hunters knew was essential for good hunting in the winter.

The lowest depths of agricultural despair occasioned Old Frustrated to read in the Farm Bulletin that one way to stop such a coon invasion was with the use of sulfur. Sulfur! That sounded like the drug that once cured me of scarlet fever!

When I professed interest in this little tidbit, I found right away that I should have remained mute. In a twinkling he told me all about it and then suggested I give it a try. I took this in like a dare. My competitive spirit was aroused, and I thereupon took it upon myself to become the savior of the corn crop and, therefore, the heroine of Hell Hole Swamp—the dumbest sucker ever born!

Often I look back on that morning, as I am doing now, and speculate about what could have led me into such folly. But try it I did. The next day found me with Number-One Boy, Diji, setting out to save the day—with sulfur. Our directions from The Great White Planter went something like this: "First, find several old bath towels, lay them flat on the ground and sprinkle liberally with powdered sulfur." (Someone else must have thought of this on another occasion, because I found an entire case of sulfur in the storeroom!) Once sprinkled, the directions continued: "Safety-pin the towel together so the sulfur will stay in place. Then take a match and light the bath towel so it will smolder. Then drag the lighted, stinking, smoking thing around the perimeter of the field."

Surely he was kidding! I would like to note that this was a huge field, bounded by blackberries and barbed wire, and he was not kidding. This caper was the result of some unknown wise person who had concluded that raccoons hated the smell of sulfur. Well, no one ever said that there was anything stupid about raccoons! Sulfur does have an odious smell! We hated it too, if you want to know the truth. As simple, and as ridiculous, as this might sound, Diji and I spent most of that morning trying to perfect the sulfur treatment procedure. We were met with at least ten problems that hampered our success. The chief concern we faced was how to keep the towel from catching in the briars and how to keep the towel on fire. It was a losing battle, and we finally gave up in disgust and withdrew to take up less malodorous duties. My recommendation, for anyone who might suffer under the delusion that this is a how-to treatise, is to forget anything you have read on the subject, immediately—including this.

Farming is an awesome profession, but it has occurred to me that perhaps we should try home-grown beef. Now that's food for thought.

Oh, What a Fowl Life

One sunny day I found Richard cleaning out the old duck pens with great vigor. This was cause for special notice, because cleaning and vigor rarely were associated with our Richard. Upon further investigation, Richard informed us that he had heard that "if you went to the post office, you could get baby chicks." With a momentary mental picture of the Postmistress of Huger surrounded by hundreds of chickens, I went on to explain to him that the only way that could happen would be for someone to have ordered chicks. This seemed to satisfy him, but he went right back to work on the pens. This led me to believe that chickens were next on his agenda, and, therefore, mine.

Quietly, I phoned The Saint and informed him of Richard's fowl-based activities, and he said he thought it was time for him to bring home a surprise. Meanwhile, back at the pens, Richard had disappeared. Disappearance was his strongest aptitude. The next thing I knew, the pens held twelve white hens and one rooster! Now how in the world did Richard do that? I thought that, most assuredly, he knew something about post offices that I did not. Ah, sweet mystery of Richard's life!

The truth was that he had made a deal with yet another friend of ours, Father Bernard, who resided at Mepkin Abbey, a neighboring plantation, which is a chicken-growing, egg-producing Trappist monastery. It seemed that a rooster had appeared in the henhouse at Mepkin, which evidently is a big faux pas in the realm of henhouses. Being sympathetic to Richard's hen-hankering, Father Bernard had donated not only the rooster, but twelve hens as well. (What are friends for?) In the afternoon, Father Bernard himself arrived to check on things at the chicken pen. It was then that I found myself in what was surely a unique circumstance for me. I sat in my chair, with Richard beside me, riveted in fascination for half an hour as a Trappist monk discussed, with fervor and in detail, the sex cycle of a chicken!

Well, Richard named each chicken, and I was greeted the next morning with a shriek of excitement: "Mom! Mom! Arthur laid an egg!" And sure enough, not only had Arthur done such a good deed, but so had Geraldine, Henrietta, George and the others. We were in the egg business.

Just to keep things on their usual even keel, St. Nick did come home with a surprise: a box full of baby chicks, five ducklings, and two baby turkeys. No peacocks? He always does things in such extremes. We already had Arthur!

I thought it quite amazing, but inevitable, that everything, animate or inanimate, ended up on The Patio. In this case, it was no different. According to the usual practice, it was not too long before we had the whole kit and caboodle of chickenhood living right outside the living room door. The ponies sneered, but Rip, our lovely golden retriever, in his good-natured, quiet way, was the greatest help when these noisy little creatures strayed. We christened him our own cotton-pickin' chicken-sitter. He was always so nice about everything. The little ones loved his fur and would walk all over him, hunting and pecking. Rip would roll his eyes to heaven as if to say, "First those creepy ponies and now this humiliation . . . why me, Lord?" But, patient as always, he would lie very still.

Like Rip, I too asked, "Why me, Lord?" and with good reason. Richard was most knowledgeable about animals and their ways, but I always felt he didn't quite believe in animal instinct. He was forever trying to teach a bird to fly, a chicken to scratch, or in this instance, a duck to swim. He had rigged a nice swimming place for the new young ducks in an old ice cooler (on The Patio), and the little ones seemed quite happy with paddling round and round in the old ice bucket. Then Richard went off to swim in the new pond himself.

But disaster lurked. Upon his return from the pond he was faced with the unpleasant task of removing five drowned ducks from the cooler! They had splashed and played so much that the water level had become too low to let them get out of the cooler when they were tired. The only recourse left for them was to sink to the bottom and stand there. Ghastly! I shuddered as it occurred to me that our first pig had starved to death (his companion pig was a bigger pig), two cows (so far) had died from being stuck in the mud and four were struck by lightning. I hate to mention the bull, who literally blew up from eating fermented soybeans! Now we had drowned five ducks. The mortality rate at Limerick was not what one would call commendable.

At this point, St. Nick entered the picture wholeheartedly. Not about to knuckle under to anything like a high mortality rate, he came home the next day with thirty-two mallard ducklings. They were too young to live outside, so they were put in the laundry room to nurture. Young mallards are marked so beautifully, and we found them fun to watch. But, alas, this group was to be with us only a few short weeks. While we were taking Diji to boarding school in Tennessee, all of those little ducks mysteriously died. We had left them under the care of a young neighbor girl who had promised to look after them while we were gone. Poor things! Upon finding the results of this duck plague, she took things into her own hands. When we returned, we were greeted immediately with a foul odor, which was readily traced. On the kitchen counter was a shoebox tied with string and neatly labeled, "Thirty-two dead ducks, one turkey. I am sorry." A more succinct message could never have been penned!

Now the duck war was on. Old Plentiful grabbed the bull by the horns, so to speak, and came home the next day with nineteen larger mallards. Surely he could not tempt fate with larger ducks. The problem of duck survival was truly met this time, but another problem developed, wherein The Saint gained yet another name. We now called him Mother Goose! These ducks had decided that they definitely preferred The Patio to the pond—any pond—and would not stay in the water—any water—at all. Mother Goose and Richard spent an entire weekend herding this little clutch of mallards towards the rice fields. With long stick in hand, Old M.G. would maneuver the ducks to the water's edge and then fling them into the pond, along with a few epithets. They would never hit the water! No, sir. Making that lovely silken sound that whirring duck wings can make, they would make a picturesque circle over the pond and head right back to The Patio. Old Mother Goose walked at least ten miles during that weekend, while I marveled that ducks could fly in air that was so blue! Eventually, they stayed. Lots of eggs hatched in the spring, most of which were eaten by other varmints, a red-tailed hawk in particular. We were able to hatch only two in an incubator. I felt that two out of twenty-four was not a very good average, but par for our course. Our life with fine feathered fowl friends had become foul, indeed. It wasn't difficult at this time to conclude that our raising ducks was "for the birds."

My Life Is a
Many-Splendor'd Thing

During the time we lived at Limerick, I can remember thinking that, other than living fifty miles from town, we lived a life that was pretty normal for our "time in life." Saint Dad was a mortgage banker and went to his office every day. I was a housewife and stayed home to keep house, mend socks and entertain on the weekends. The four children went to four different schools and had homework to do each night, and we had pets to look after and chores to do, just like everyone else. How perfectly normal! My life, because we lived at Limerick, was a many-splendor'd thing. But perhaps I could recognize some differences from the norm here and there.

That might be what led me to take the time to jot down the following schedule lo these many years ago. I don't remember doing it, but I remember the day clearly. I will pass it on exactly as I found it on a piece of notebook paper in a desk drawer. The reader can draw his or her own conclusion re: splendor'd and normal.

7:00 a.m.	Get up, fix breakfast, pack lunches
7:30 a.m.	Drive to town. Drop each child at school (45 miles)
8:45 a.m.	Be at Miss Mason's School as driver for trip (10 miles)
11:00 a.m.	Coffee with friend
11:30 a.m.	Drive to Rent-All to see about a sander (5 miles)
12:30 p.m.	Lunch with Nick (The Saint)
1:30 p.m.	Get hamburger for Courtenay
2:00 p.m.	Go to three schools to see about tuitions (5 miles)
3:00 p.m.	Pick up sander across the Ashley River (5 miles)
3:15 p.m.	Pick up Richard at Miss Mason's after sports (5 miles)
4:00 p.m.	Drive back home with children and sander (45 miles)
4:15 p.m.	Try to put paper on sander. Succeed at 5:15 p.m.
5:30 p.m.	See how sander is working
5:45 p.m.	Make bread pudding
6:00 p.m.	See about homework
6:10 p.m.	Drive to town for choir practice (45 miles)
7:00 p.m.	Choir practice—singing Handel
7:10 p.m.	Elizabeth can't find Dad. Wants to go home
8:30 p.m.	Drive home (45 miles)
9:15 p.m.	Must walk in because a car is parked on cattle guard
9:30 p.m.	Find very drunk visitor looking for her runaway daughter. Liquor cabinet is empty
10:00 p.m.	Ride bike to gate to bring her car to house
10:30 p.m.	Take her home (6 miles)
10:45 p.m.	Errant Dad returns from birthday party, much celebrated—with Elizabeth
11:00 p.m.	Fix scrambled eggs for husband. Forget bread pudding
11:20 p.m.	Quiet in house. Piano sonata on while I read
12:30 a.m.	Go to bed
6:00 a.m.	Call from drunk friend . . . has found her daughter
7:00 a.m.	Fix breakfast . . .

The Point

On some days, when things became too fraught with the daily demand on an already frenetic housewife, I would, if at all possible, say, "Phooey. I'll just go down to The Point and watch the river." I could fix a sandwich for me and one for my dog Bobo, and we two kindred spirits would escape.

I loved that walk to The Point, and my route rarely deviated: down past the flowing well, across the bank between the Fish Pond and the Boys' Pond, around the Big Rice Fields and on down to The Point, where the Cooper River idled by.

From The Point, on various occasions, I have seen the sun set in a shower of gold, and I have seen the sun rise, fighting its way through the morning mists. But to see it enveloped in the honey glow of a full moon is probably the finest sight in Christendom. Whatever the time of day or time of year, this lovely spot has always worked miracles for me.

As I walked, it was not long before I found myself in that "other" world . . . undisturbed by civilization. This was a world of sunshine, fresh breezes and the incessant hum of thousands of bees. I was aware of nothing but sounds and scents and peace . . . so often absent from nearly everyone's lives.

Upon reaching The Point, I settled down on a soft clump of grass to watch the swift current swirl by. On this day, the tide was going out . . . towards Charleston. The Point, as we called it, has many stories to tell about this part of the East Branch of the Cooper River.

When the tide is low, piles of bricks and old timbers protrude from the mud, as this was near an old dock at Limerick. I could just imagine the schooners, sails furled, navigating the currents and the bends of the river as they came to load barrels of rice.

To my right were remnants of a long, straight canal, which at one time was the rail bed of a small-gauge railroad on which phosphate—a natural fertilizer, found on an inland part of the property in the nineteenth century—could be moved to the dock on the river.

On the other side of the creek, beyond the canal, an Indian Mound rose to a lofty pinnacle. "Pinnacle" is surely the wrong term in the Lowcountry, as is "lofty," but anyway, in prehistoric times, Native Americans created this man-made hill for purposes believed to be ceremonial. It was a wonderful place to sit, very still, hidden against a tree, to wait and watch deer go to the creek to drink.

This river has clearly played a part in our lives, and today the memories clamored for my attention.

Sometimes, after too much rain, the river would flood and the current would sweep by The Point at breakneck speed. Ofttimes, during such floods, the children would go over to the boat landing at the site of Huger's Bridge and jump in to whirl with the current, bobbing and screeching with delight. When they came around the bend and reached The Point, they would grab an overhanging limb and climb out. I did this with them once, and discovered that it truly was exciting, because the current was so fast and furious. Only in retrospect did I realize the danger in this escapade, and what would have happened if anyone had missed the limb! Ah, youth—theirs and mine!

I remember another time during an even larger flood, when the water seemed to cover all of lower Limerick. I went down the hill for a closer look. It was fascinating to see how flooded-out creatures had scrambled for safety. Every leaf and high branch was covered with those insects and animals who had lost their homes to the flood. Just then an unusual sound reached my ears, getting louder with each passing moment. It sounded like a waterfall. I could see nothing to account for it, and I just could not imagine what kind of rushing water was headed my way. It was eerie. I was concerned enough to think I should move to higher ground, even though I couldn't imagine just what waters had broken loose from what. Just then, around the curve in the bank came ten cows, side by side, like a row of Roman chariots. Evidently they had been separated from the others by the flood while down at The Point and were now trying to join the rest of the herd. With each of the combined steps of these huge animals, they pushed the water aside in an enormous slosh. The sound of that swishing water was prodigious. That is a wonderful memory.

And then there was the winter when we had a very hard freeze, extremely unusual for our region. It was so cold that the river froze over—at high tide. A shelf of ice formed . . . not strong enough to walk on, of course, but it made a skating rink for the ducks and other wintry waterfowl. As the tide went out, the ice remained, hanging, and we could hear the crash of this frozen river falling into itself all day along. This was another captivating memory of The Point.

The Point was the camping place for many a brave and daring youngster during our years at Limerick. One favorite camping expedition occurred when The Saint and several of his Hunting Buddies invited their daughters to camp out . . . no brothers, only girls and dads. The girls were all excited and were far more industrious than the boys in erecting their tents, gathering firewood for the campfire, and helping the dads rig a trotline across the river. They had been instructed that they would be eating whatever they caught. They were not so enthusiastic when the majority of the catch on the trotline was a mess of eels! The mere mention of scrambled eggs and eel wrings strong reactions from these young ladies to this day.

As a pair of herons flew by, a lovely white blur, I was stirred to reflect on how physically different The Point and the surrounding woodlands were from the woods in which we had played during my childhood days in Kentucky. With its steep hills, outcroppings of limestone and bubbling, coursing creek racing through at the bottom, those woods were quite the opposite of this area known as Hell Hole Swamp. Yet in its beauty and wild tranquility, those Kentucky woods were just the same. My love and appreciation for such solitude remain with me to this day, no matter where I might be.

Have You Ever Touched an Alligator?

Have you ever touched an alligator? Ever wanted to touch one? I didn't think so.

From the first day of my residence in South Carolina I knew that alligators were indigenous to these parts, along with quite a few other reptilians that I would just as soon have ignored. This was schoolbook knowledge, bearing no relation to my real life that was to be. However, when one resided in Hell Hole Swamp, all the above knowledge became very real and personal. Snakes and alligators were close neighbors, and like it or not, sooner or later, one of those spurned creatures was bound to make an appearance. I remember a bright summer's day at Limerick that catapulted me into the category of one who has touched an alligator.

It was a typical midsummer day at Limerick. The boys had company for the weekend. The Saint was plowing, I was mowing, and all and sundry were having fun, when a loud cry went up, "Alligator!" Even though we knew they were around and could hear them bellowing at night, we rarely actually saw alligators because they are so well camouflaged. The cry from the boys came once more, and attention was paid to Diji and his friend, who were at the bottom of the hill at the canal of the Boys' Pond. The Saint was nearby, and I could see all from The Patio. The boys continued to shout and point at the water. It was an alligator all right, about four-and-a-half feet long and cruising up and down the canal, bold as you please. Most all of us converged on the scene to see the alligator. This was exciting! Usually alligators are skittish and don't let you see them. This was also a period when alligators had been placed on the Endangered Species List, which implied we had even less chance of seeing them. I, for one, was certainly a novice at alligatorism. The Saint's father, Old Bwana, had filled my Cum Ya ears with tall tales of alligators the size of giant whales, of how to distinguish their deep croaks from those of bullfrogs, and how the danger in such critters was not so much from the mouth, which looked fierce enough, but from the swishing of the tail, which, he said, could break the leg of a grown man. In other words, don't mess with an alligator. I took these words as gospel, so I had no intention of doing such messing, but the boys were excited and The Saint was right there to protect us all. Thus lulled into security, we all gathered round to stare at the creature in our lagoon.

Not one to be lulled into anything, The Saint did not like the idea of having such a beast trespassing in our canal so close to the house. We had already lost one dog, presumably swallowed by this alligator's cousin, Fang, so with his inimitable way of reasoning, The Saint lifted his ever-handy shotgun and shot this alligator. "Take that!" was the message, loud and clear. The alligator sank out of sight into the murky water of the canal. Sinking out of sight is what they do best. Then, with no hesitation whatsoever, The Saint put down his gun, took his cigarettes out of his pocket and jumped in after the alligator! One shot and he jumps in. How in the world would one know if he hit the right spot? I expected to see the water roil with the alligator's wrath at such treatment, but nothing like that occurred, and just as quickly, up Young Bwana came, with the alligator in his arms. Aghast, we all watched, totally in awe of the spectacle at hand.

Well, Old Jungle Jim handed the prize over to Diji and his friend, and they carried it up to the house and laid it out on the stone table on The Patio. What a sight! We could never have got so close to any animal at a zoo, so we moved in for a good look-see. This is where my earlier question originated: "Have you ever touched an alligator?" Of course we never had, so touch we did.

He was made just like a coat of armor, with overlapping plates of hard shell-like material, with sharp ridges running down his back. His eyes poked up high so he could submerge and still keep his eyes above water, as did his nostrils. I immediately was reminded of Captain Hook and his mean old crocodile. Yes, this was a fascinating thing to be doing, I thought, as I rapped him on his side and heard the clank echo across The Patio. We all stood there in silent awe at this armored specimen from our own watery deep. I was just about to make some comment about his thick hide when, blink, blink, the alligator's eye popped wide open and looked straight at me. Yikes! He most definitely was not dead. His mouth was damaged and he did not move. I thought this to be a good thing, but that didn't mean that he wouldn't move! We all stepped back.

"Well, now you've gone and done it," I railed at The Saint. "What now? What are we to do with it?"

An answer was slow in coming. What were we to do with it? Alligators were on the endangered species list, for starters. Mum was the word. Since an answer was not immediately forthcoming, The Saint gathered up the alligator and put in our Mud Room bathtub. That should hold him while we think of an answer, was the train of thought of that moment. I was still reeling over having touched a live alligator.

Before too long, Old Croc Killer had come up with a solution. I never will fathom how he knows such things, but he made a phone call to some Hell Hole Swamp alligator bootleggers. Yes, there were such things just a phone call away! They said they would take the beast off our hands and not report us if we would let them hunt other like kind in our canals that night. These were rough characters. We gave quick assent to their suggestions. Our alligator lolled in the bathtub until this took place.

That evening, I felt rather certain that we might be among the very few who had ever seen illegal alligator hunters at work—and lived to tell of it. They were serious about their task. Before climbing into the canal, where I wouldn't go in broad daylight, these men donned waders and wore miner's hats with lights attached at the forehead. This, I was told, allowed them to see the reflections of the eyes of their prey—remember, alligator eyes shine back red—while keeping their hands free for the catching. To this day, I cannot see how anyone would willingly go wading in those canals at night hoping to drag an alligator from its lair. Who's to say a cottonmouth might not get in the way? Ugh! Such silly thoughts never entered the heads of these tough men, so off they went.

They came back empty-handed, I fear, so I suppose it was a good thing for them that they already had our alligator as a trophy. I guess it was also a good thing that we had escaped the scourge of being criminals for damaging an endangered species. Whew!

Again I ask, "Have you ever touched an alligator?"

Scarlett Doesn't Live Here Anymore

To have been resettled into the South Carolina Lowcountry was, indubitably, one of the most delightful things to occur in my life, and when, in due course, I was so fortunate as to be able to move to such a pretty place as Limerick Plantation, it changed my life forevermore!

In spite of the excitement of everyday life there, I loved living at Limerick inordinately. Most people were interested to hear we lived on a plantation, but through the years, I noticed that in non-plantation dwellers there was a certain romanticized idea of plantations and the life thereon. As a Certified Tour Guide of the Lowcountry, whose responsibility it was to impart pertinent historic information to interested travelers on a regular basis, I have seen eyes light up at the mention of the word "plantation," and it was very clear that the influence of Margaret Mitchell was far-reaching and utterly pervasive. Those visitors, the Cum Ya's of the outside tour world, envisioned life on a plantation today much as it would have been in the days of Scarlett, Rhett, and Ashley, complete with mint juleps on the porch and Mammy in the kitchen. I wish I had a penny for everyone who has asked me where Rhett Butler was buried!

Even when one was keenly aware of the truth, the Tara vision could be contagious, especially when there was a plantation available. Imagination can be awesome when left to wander freely, so on one balmy afternoon, while sitting on The Patio, even I let this idea get the best of me, and I embarked on a fantastic daydream—but was it a dream?

The fantasy of elegant antebellum plantation living here at Limerick hit a snag almost immediately for lots of reasons, but firstly because there was no Mammy in the kitchen, or anywhere else for that matter. There was a Mom, but due to the urgencies of daily demands unknown to Scarlett, culinary expertise was often limited to cans and boxes. The proverbial mint juleps could be managed, silver cups and all, but who really likes mint juleps? However, if one might substitute a bit of gin and tonic in the julep cup, one could sit on The Patio, enjoy the view, and escape malaria all at the same time. Come to think about it, I don't believe, then or now, there could be any better pastime in the world than to sit with a loved one at twilight, viewing the rice fields at Limerick Plantation with a julep cup of gin and tonic in hand and a faithful golden retriever at your feet.

Rice fields themselves are a tonic. It has always been my hope that someday, somewhere, I will get to see a field full of golden, ripening rice. In the meantime, I am content with pigweed and water hyacinths, and enjoy the colors as the greenery, reflected in the watery ponds, varies with each move of the sun, creating a constantly changing waterscape, inhabited by untold varieties of birds and waterfowl. But I digress.

Back to my romantic interlude, where another hurdle for the imagery of the past was the porch. We didn't have one of those either, but we did have The Patio. Its location was strategically placed so as to enhance the doing of what I was just describing, but I am quite sure that Miss Scarlett and Rhett would have preferred the haven of their own portico to my patio. In any case, I am hard pressed to re-create the atmosphere of antebellum Tara at Limerick. Although the view is unsurpassed, it is difficult to drift into romantic reverie while two raccoons are trying to steal the ice out of the julep cup. This is but one of the impediments.

Usually, at reverie time, my pastoral scene of green pastures full of grazing cattle come to life and the cows decide that their pastoral idyll is better composed in my front yard. Watching this gentle group of bovines quietly chewing their way into view, I remembered that when I was studying in England, in particular about the great landscape designer Capability Brown, I read that he referred to his bucolic, English, cow-filled countryside as "an animated landscape." This took on added meaning at Limerick. My animated landscape took over my plantation life, driving me to constant cow-chasing, coon-chasing and other animal capers that took place much too close to my front door.

To add to the confusion and further distract me from romantic reverie, this time of day brought not only cows and coons to the sanctity of The Patio, but also children, whose lives seemed to depend on bouncing tennis balls off the chimney, and ducks who wanted to play in the freshly stomped flower beds. Reverie time or not, it was about this time that I deemed it wiser to give the gin to the raccoons and retreat into the house to become a short-order cook.

However, romantic notions never leave the head entirely. Along with the ideas outlined above, there arises the equally picturesque daydream of dashing figures galloping up on stupendous white chargers, and of ladies who always, as heroines of novels, poems and histories, are endowed with equestrian grace. This, then, must be why I was so often asked, "Of course, you have horses at Limerick, don't you?" It was difficult to ascertain whether it was a question or a statement, but everyone, I mean everyone, expected us to have horses. Well, we didn't. After the pony episode, I was the first to admit that the thought of more horseflesh had not been entertained with any enthusiasm. Nevertheless, if you had a plantation, then, by golly, you were supposed to ride out every morning, before breakfast, to look over the South Forty, and in the evening, you were supposed to go on exciting rides with a handsome gallant. They did this in all the books! It was a beautiful, romantic idea, one to which we succumbed that very summer.

Daydreaming aside, we acquired two horses. They were two very tall horses, and neither had ever heard of Scarlett O'Hara or Limerick Plantation.

At this point in my daydream, it may be important to remind one and all that my roots were in Kentucky, the horse capital of our nation. As a youngster, I can remember saving every cent of my baby-sitting earnings to ride on the bridle trails near my home. I, too, begged for a horse when I was about thirteen, but the most my father ever produced was an ex-circus horse, thirty-five-dollar variety, who had a propensity for walking on his hind legs at unannounced moments. I can assure you that this sort of thing did nothing to help me achieve equestrian style. Also, at that time in my life, I was madly in love with a gorgeous boy who was winning all the blue ribbons at horse shows in Louisville, taking several ribbons at Madison Square Garden to boot. From him, I picked up some of the lingo of horsemanship, so in my mind, I felt just as "in" as any of my horsy, fox-hunting friends—maybe even more so. I do think that having Kentucky in one's background commands a certain amount of prestige in the world of horses, but then, I may be biased.

To get back to the subject at hand, yes, if I wanted to continue with the antebellum fantasy of plantation life, then we needed those two very tall horses. And I needed to play the part of Southern belle, or so I thought.

Our household was very excited when they learned that we had bought two horses from a young friend who was leaving for college. It was a shame, everyone said, that these horses would no longer be ridden, so to Limerick they did come. Ooh, but they were big horses! They seemed twice as tall as I was. Big or not, I was determined that I should gain equestrian grace and join the ranks of all those romantic figures of old, even if it killed me. How prophetic were those thoughts. It wasn't long before I knew that the odds and the gods were all against me.

Aesthetically, the idea of a brisk ride to the South Forty appealed to me and didn't seem to be out of the realm of possibility. Since there was no Mammy in the kitchen cooking up hominy and biscuits, this Mom could not go riding until after breakfast. And another very real difficulty developed in the plan. Having no barn and few fences, I was forced to walk to the South Forty just to catch the horses! This took half the fun out of it, especially since I had to drag the saddle with me. Once at the South Forty, which was really the East Twenty, I found it no easy trick to catch my stupendous steed. All I had been told by the previous owner, who was a beautiful rider, was that if I whistled and beat on a bucket, these fine, tall horses would come immediately. Ha! I have never been able to whistle the proper way, but I gave it my all, while beating furiously on a bucket. My entourage of young people and dog assisted as best they could. Even so, it took, with the help of Diji and Richard, a minimum of forty-five minutes to lay one hand on the first horse. It took another thirty minutes to get the saddle on securely. By then, I was pretty tired, but I had not yet lost interest. Whew!

I then summoned all my powers of concentration towards

mounting yon steed, and then riding into antebellum oblivion as envisioned in my daydreams. My, but those were tall horses! If I thought catching this horse was hard, then this mounting operation was ridiculous! My short legs, attached as they were to a frame that was somewhat pudgier than that of my Kentucky youth, found that they just were not up to it. Let's face it—the seventeen-inch waist never existed! After too lengthy a time, I finally succeeded in getting one foot in the stirrup. The horse, so encumbered with this short, prickly burr of a person, was no help at all. Wanting nothing to do with me, he took off at quite a fast clip. The resulting effect was nothing short of astonishing. I, the mother of four, the mistress of a vast plantation, a native of Kentucky yet, was reduced to utter degradation. Already attached to the horse by one leg in the stirrup, I found that I was now making colossal, twenty-foot, one-legged bunny hops across the pasture while frantically, and unsuccessfully, trying to heave myself into the saddle. I decided it necessary, really imperative, to get on that horse or be drawn and quartered right in front of the children. It must have been that terrible thought that spurred me on, because somehow I did it. I was on top! In the saddle! Ooh, what a tall horse he was!

With most of the battle now won, I swallowed hard, waved to the children, and tally-ho'd, trying with all my might to concentrate on equestrian grace. And then I was off—not off to the races, but off as in not on the back of the horse! It took no more than twenty seconds for me to be off, sailing through the air, landing in a heap at the feet of my children. The horse looked at me with practically a sneer. "I know your kind," he seemed to say. Not to be outdone by a mere horse, even a tall one, I let him know I was from Kentucky! I repeated the procedure over and over again, day after day. The longest I ever stayed on was two minutes. By the end of the third day, I had been brushed off by a multitude of trees, been thrown sixteen times and fallen once when the saddle came loose. There was hardly a piece of me that was not battered and bruised.

The children were positive they were to be motherless very soon, and the horse and others at home had that scornful air of "I told you so" about them.

What had happened to all my Kentucky equestrian grace? I called my mother and cried out my tale of pain and woe, and she answered me with a wisdom mothers always seemed to have. "You silly goose," she admonished. "Surely you must remember that you never came home with the horse. Stay off those horses, especially at your age." Yes, a sage was my mother! I had conveniently forgotten those long, horseless walks back to the stable. Well, at that moment I couldn't even walk to the kitchen where Mammy wasn't! So I took her advice and gave up riding. I was game for lots, but this type of punishment was more than even I deserved. And the "at your age" comment was very hurtful. Worst of all, a handsome gallant never materialized! I supposed that meant that I must be content with The Saint, who is no great horseman himself and was only very rarely gallant!

The horses were relegated to running wild once more, where they took up cow-chasing as a hobby, as had their predecessors. When we began getting phone calls that the horses had leaped the cattle guard and eaten the experimental gardens in the National Forest across the road, the decision was easily made to give them away. They were sent to another neighboring plantation, which was equipped for such folly, and my dreams of equestrian grace were laid to rest. As for Scarlett and Rhett . . . I really didn't "give a damn"!

Wilbur

With all that talk of *Gone With the Wind*, I remember how I loved the movie's great barbecue scene at Twelve Oaks. Now that was a party to which I, a century-plus later, could relate. Plantations and barbecues are legendary companions. Limerick fit right into that picture—well, sort of.

It's funny how one's mind works. I passed a sign one day that caught my attention. In great big red letters were emblazoned the words, "Custom Slaughtering." I have seen that sign on numerous occasions, but this time, it struck my funny bone. Somehow, I had never thought about a slaughterhouse in the same way I would a tailor's shop. It rather put the slaughterhouse in the world inhabited by the Mafia, which, in turn, reminded me of how we had put out a contract on our pig, Wilbur. He was headed towards Custom Slaughtering for sure. Maybe pigs go by the eat-drink-and-be-merry philosophy. But I have often wondered what it would be like to be a Wilbur, and know that your prime reason for being was eventually not to be. I shall not dwell on that thought.

Wilbur came to reside at our house, not at my invitation, but because St. Nick and The Hunting Buddies wanted to have a real barbecue. It was no fun to go to ordinary barbecues, because it was not the real stuff. What constituted "real" to them was to stay up all night to tend the coals and to administer the Rites of Realness to whatever had been the result of Custom Slaughtering.

Poor Wilbur. He had been in the wrong place at the wrong time, a half-grown piglet who just happened along—or so they said—one day while the boys were deer hunting. He also just happened not to have a mother in sight, and we just happened to have a pen at Limerick in which the poor little orphan could take refuge. (That is how it was explained to me.) If all went according to the plans of The Hunting Buddies, a few months of careful ministrations would render Wilbur ready for sacrificial offering, thereby satisfying the desire for a real barbecue. This also signaled that a real party was in the offing. One could only hope it might be as grand a party as the one at Twelve Oaks! As it was, by the end of those intervening months, I was ready to offer myself for Custom Slaughtering!

Life at Limerick at that time was already topsy-turvy since we were adding two rooms to the house. This was also the time in my life that the ponies, ducks, chickens, dogs and a calf all had taken up residence on The Patio. I drew the line at a having a pig on The Patio! So Wilbur was secured in the dog pen. I did not especially enjoy the thought of having the house overlook a picturesque pigpen, but it was closer for carrying food than any other alternative. Also, the pen was very large, with running water, and it had a house in it, so life in such a fine porky condo should be rosy for Wilbur. All we had to do was feed him and watch him grow.

It was not difficult to deduce who was to be the chief feeder of Wilbur. Because of this, I found myself to be in the closest of relationships with him. He loved me! And, try as I might, I could not help getting to know him. But Wilbur *was* a pig. Before long, he taught me first and foremost that which I never knew until then: I hate being jumped on by a pig! Because of this, I hated to carry that bucket of slop down to him every day. I was taught, early in my life, never to say "hate," but here I had to make an exception.

In the meantime efforts were concentrated, with renewed diligence, on finishing off Wilbur to the perfection expected for the real barbecue. So carry I did, and jumped on I was . . . every day. The dogs were jealous, to an extreme, always making the chore more difficult. The ponies were worse. Wilbur was always overanxious and therefore got most of himself into the bucket before I could get the contents into the trough, resulting in my being bathed in slop and stepped upon by Wilbur. I tried all sorts of tricks, but he was too smart. I hate being covered in pig slop!

Pigs are smart. Wilbur was no exception, and he became skilled in an infinite number of things designed to drive me crazy, the worst of which was learning how to open the gate of the dog pen. Now that was serious. He learned the combination to every gate fastener we tried, and when loose in the outside world, he came to look for you-know-who! I hate being followed by a pig!

I was beginning to get a complex about Wilbur's following me everywhere, even fishing. I shuddered at the thought of anyone seeing me fishing with a pig in attendance, but even if I could get him back in the pen, he wouldn't stay. There was no way I could get him to behave, either. If he wanted the chicken feed, then he would take the chicken feed. The problem with that was that the chicken feed was in the laundry room! I hate having pigs in my house!

I soon felt that the whole of my every day was spent trying to ditch Wilbur. It wasn't long before I began to envision Wilbur on the dining table, with an apple in his mouth. I reveled in these visions. When strangers asked how we could possibly entertain the thought of eating our pet, I was quick to answer, "Just you watch!"

All came to a head one afternoon in June, and I nearly lost

my head! On this day the children were all involved in some extracurricular activity, so I returned from the city alone. Within two minutes, I discovered that Wilbur had made good his escape and, of course, had made his inevitable run for The Patio. Not finding me to bother, he had turned to finer things and had located a fifty-pound bag of dog food leaning against the chimney. With typical pig gusto, he was now up to his shoulders in manna from dog heaven. He was so excited that he didn't even bother to raise his head to greet me, his main benefactor. A bad-mannered pig, indeed!

The dogs also had become excited about the ripped-open bag of dog goodies, and in spite of their distaste for Wilbur, they joined him in assaulting the heap of tasty morsels spilling all over The Patio. All manner of whoops and hollering from me had no effect in stopping the melee. In fact, I only seemed to make things worse.

The frog gig was leaning nearby, so, in my frustration, I grabbed it and went at Wilbur with the sharp end. I'm quite sure that I know few in this world who have ever tried to gig a pig. Don't bother! Wilbur was impervious to any and all insults to his body and continued snorting his way towards complete pig obesity. I felt helpless—and mad. This was unusual, because I rarely did mad. But I was mad to the boiling point because I was frustrated.

In his frantic lunging, and perhaps because of the gig, I will never really know, Wilbur backed up and bumped the picnic table behind him, hitting it with the force of a tank. He was as big as a tank. That in itself was not so horrible, but on that table rested a large bottle—a glass bottle—a glass bottle full of concentrated bug poison. The operative word here was "concentrated." The next few seconds seemed to hang in the air as though an hour had passed. I watched, frozen, mouth agape, as, in absolute slow motion, that bottle wobbled back and forth; it turned on its base; it tipped up, up, and over; then slowly, oh, so slowly, it fell, end over end, finally crashing to the concrete floor of The Patio. There, with an immense crash and splash, the jar broke into a million pieces and the gooey liquid inside began to spread—oh, so slowly—over the step and oozed its way out into the middle of the patio and into the dog food mess Wilbur had created.

I was thunderstruck. The pig began to slip, and was soon on his back in the puddle of poison, which now was soaking into the dog food the dogs were eating. Wilbur wiggled there, his feet flailing as he tried to regain his footing. This was a horror story. I had to do something quick—anything—so I did. After the frog gig fizzle, the most logical, and the next handiest thing available to me in that horrible moment, was the hose. Aha! Without another thought, I turned it on, ready to wash it all away, thereby ending the problem. Wrong! Concentrated—remember? In less than twenty seconds, I had succeeded in making at least a hundred gallons of poison! By now, the puddle covered most of the patio and was running off the edges into the flower beds. The ducks were trying to swim in it! This was truly a disaster in the making. The pig was undeterred as he slipped once more onto his back in the ooze. The dogs had eaten poisoned food and the ducks were swimming in liquid poison. There was no correcting this error! It was a calamity!

At this point, all I could think to do was pray. I prayed that the loathsome pig would willingly go back to his pen. I prayed that the dogs had not eaten too much tainted food and I prayed that the feathered friends could somehow overcome what was bound to overcome them. Mostly, I prayed fervently to be rid of this pig.

Even so, I hosed off Wilbur the best I could and finally maneuvered him, back to his abode at the bottom of the hill. I then put the dogs in the shower and left them there with the water running. My frustrated flutterings scared the ducks away for the moment. I was in quite a state myself. I hate days like this!

In desperation, I then called The Vet, who clucked his tongue in a most obnoxious way, intimating that he thought he had heard everything until now. He then prescribed a tablespoon of hydrogen peroxide for each dog. "Hydrogen peroxide?" I wailed. "That's poison!" I knew that when I put it on cut knees it bubbled like a witch's cauldron and killed germs. I was sure it would kill my dogs too. He explained that it would not, and forcefully bade me get on with it.

The two dogs were Rip, the old cotton-pickin' chicken-sitter, and his younger colleague, Beauregard, sometimes called "Bo-regardless" by Diji. Two more sweet, lovable, adorable, obedient, perfect dogs did not exist in this world, and I was going to kill them. Groan. Woe. I hate killing my loved ones!

Obediently, the dogs sat still as statues while I administered what I was sure to be a lethal dose of medicine. How I despised that pig! Bobo and Rip just looked at me soulfully with their great big brown eyes, and then, one by one, they began to burp. There was no nice word for it. But these were not ordinary burps. These dogs were burping bubbles! Both dogs looked hydrophobic. Soon the yard was full of Bobo-bubbles, and Rip was so embarrassed he went to the edge of the yard and turned his back on me. I will never forget watching that dog trying to regain his composure and self-respect while his shoulders heaved and the air floated with bubbles.

Well, it worked. Though chagrined, the dogs lived. Of course, the pig was fine, saved for another day of mayhem. The chickens and ducks were not. Well, we were used to starting over with fowl. I was still a wreck! If there was any positive consequence to this unbelievable afternoon, it was that, without question, it was a long time before a bug of any description dared come on The Patio!

Tom, Tom the piper's son
  Stole a pig and away he run—
  Tom was beat, the pig was eat . . . AND . . .

The Real Barbecue

Barbecue in the South is all-important, and anywhere you go in the South you'll find a competitive spirit amongst barbecue lovers. I say in the South because elsewhere, the term "barbecue" simply means cooking out on a grill. Those who reside in North Carolina have a special way of making their barbecue. People who reside in Macon, Georgia, are renowned for their special recipe. Kentucky has what they call barbecue, but for me it doesn't measure up, now that I have experienced so many different barbecue tastes. Barbecue in Upper South Carolina is different from Lower South Carolina. Some people like a mustard sauce, some like a vinegar sauce, some tomato, and some simply must have slaw on theirs. The differences go on and on. In other words, barbecue is a very personal thing down here, with highly localized preferences.

Because Limerick is located in the wilds of Berkeley County and an hour's drive from town, it was always assumed that any of our visitors should stay for dinner once they were there. Consequently, all our parties involved food and lots of it. (I once bought a canoe paddle in order to stir an enormous vat of venison stew I had prepared in anticipation of some big shindig.)

The desires of The Hunting Buddies and The Saint brought all this sharply into focus with the raising of Wilbur, and we wives willingly joined in to make the plans for the eating of Wilbur a reality. We would host a "real" barbecue at Limerick. We all vowed to make this the best party on record. This was to be a great family day as well, so we wanted everyone to bring children. The menu would be typical: pork (done the real way, of course), rice, a Carolina specialty called hash, baked beans and coleslaw, plus a variety of desserts. For the children we added bushels of apples. It would be a do-whatever-you-want-to-do day, with Wilbur being the pièce de résistance. As the party date approached, our workload increased. The invitations were out, and very few regrets were received. What a compliment. Then we counted heads. Horrors! The heads coming, each with a mouth to feed, numbered over a hundred. Was Wilbur up to it? Even the most careful ministrations would not stretch him that far, so hot dogs were added to the menu. Libations covered the full spectrum of enjoyment! No doubt about it . . . this would be a real fine party!

We ladies did not dispute the fact that home-cooked barbecue was better tasting. The trouble for us lay in home-cooked rice, hash and beans for that many people. This called for organization, stamina and more than one day in the kitchen. We also needed more kitchen than I had. Not only did we need to cook for one hundred–plus, but four families were to be housed and fed at Limerick for the entire weekend as well. I can assure you we endured a lot for the privilege of having that real barbecue.

As the party weekend approached, the first, and most important, chore was to take Wilbur to be customized. It took a long time to capture Wilbur, and he was a most unwilling passenger in the old

blue station wagon that took him away. Poor Wilbur. Poor me.
In spite of my remonstrations, I had become truly attached to the
old guy. I had thought I wouldn't mind, but—poor me.

The next step, after a gargantuan visit to the grocery store, was
to cook, cook, cook: rice steamers puffing, food choppers chopping
and grinding, axes chopping firewood, and the men engineering a
monumental pig cooker just off one end of The Patio.

While all this was in progress, we sent Hunting Buddy Number
One to pick up Wilbur at the custom house, which was many miles
away. Shortly thereafter, in the midst of our KP endeavors, the
phone rang. It was Hunting Buddy Number One, and his words
were awful to hear. Work slowed to a halt in the kitchen as the
look of consternation on my face showed. The conversation went
something like this:

"Liz, didn't you say the butcher had already been paid?"

"Yes. Is something wrong?"

"Check again. They say we owe them twenty-one dollars."

"You tell them to check again. We have already paid them
seventeen dollars." (Customizing Wilbur certainly was not costly.)
There was a long pause, and then,

"Oh, no!" he said. "That just can't be . . . Oh, no! Damn!"
(I expect the expletive was something different from "damn.") Then
there was silence.

"Whatever is the matter?" I screeched. The noise in the kitchen
stopped abruptly as we awaited the reply.

"Brace yourself, Liz. You won't believe this. They have cut him
up!"

"What do you mean, cut him up? Cut what up?" I felt prickly
goose bumps rising. I just couldn't absorb the problem he was
describing.

"Just what I said." His groan was audible over the phone. "Pork
chops and spare ribs!"

"Who?" I whispered.

"Wilbur!" he croaked.

"Do something, Old Buddy! Do something!" I croaked back. By now, everyone was gathered around the phone. I had visions of all of us trying to lace Wilbur back together again. One hundred and ten people—pork chops—it was an appalling thought. Minutes passed, and then the voice came back on the phone.

"False alarm, Liz." The relief could be heard in his voice. "There are two pigs here with the same last name, and Wilbur is intact!" A cheer went up for Wilbur and Big Buddy, and we all fixed a drink in celebration.

My father had a term for what we were doing—cooking and drinking at the same time. "Drooking," he called it, and that's what we proceeded to do until Hunting Buddy Number One arrived home with the goods.

On with the schedule! I was told that in order to make real barbecue hash, it was necessary to use all the unmentionable parts of the pig and then some. We girls were not very excited about this and had our own recipe, but The Saint was determined to have his way, so we sent him to the Bunk House kitchen to drook his own hash over there. He went obediently, but we couldn't help but notice that he had put a large covered pot on our stove. We found a note attached to the lid of the pot that read, "Do not open." What an invitation! One by one, we girls stealthily stole a peek into this pot, unable to resist knowing what concoction had been slipped in on us. Our reactions were united. In the pot, boiling furiously, was the head of Customized Wilbur! He was smiling! Gross! Yuck! I hate smiling pigs' heads! We didn't think much of St. Chef, either. Hogshead cheese, indeed!

One of the most significant things involved in a real barbecue was the fact that the men must stay up all night tending things. There was, necessarily, much planning, discussing and exchanging of opinions among themselves involved in such a night. The fire must be just right, the sauce (in this case vinegar-based) must be applied correctly and the pig must be turned at precisely the right times. Shifts must be drawn up and the beer iced down. All this lent an officious machismo to the pre-party atmosphere. I do not know whether it is wise to document such a night, but not to do so would deprive one of realizing how really remarkable it was that this party ever took place at all and, more importantly, just how very difficult it is to assure realness in a barbecue.

To begin with, we learned the derivation of the word "shiftless" when one of the Buddies declined his shift by falling asleep on the couch. He could not be budged. He was the subject of much kidding the next morning. Another Hunting Buddy fell off the chimney while trying to replace a light bulb. He was our first casualty, though his injury was slight. There were sleeping bodies scattered about as the nonshiftless worked through the night.

Also, since construction was under way on the house, there were several rooms without walls. One of the wives and I were relegated to sleep in such a place, and I must say it was not very private. However, it did enable us to hear the changing of the guard and the comments thereto. Those men were really funny, especially those who drooked pigs. Every time they stoked the fire in the fireplace, it was important that they let the world know they were doing it. Every time they turned Wilbur over was a time for serious discussion. All wives were summoned, no matter what time, to look and admire! The pot on the stove had finished us for looking, but they would not take no for an answer. Out we trooped into the night, leaving Shiftless, who appeared to be permanently glued to the couch, to miss all the excitement. What a sight. Each of our husbands was covered with ash. Mine was resting in the wheelbarrow, which seemed a perfect fit. Two others were leaning against the light pole in an effort to stay upright. Another was in charge and, casting an eye about, one could readily assess that his job was the hardest. Wilbur wasn't any fun to gaze upon, so we left as soon as possible.

A short time later, Hunting Buddy Number Two decided to wake up his wife. He did so in his usual quiet fashion, by lovingly swatting her on her derrière. Being aroused out of a sound sleep in such a way brought the wife bolting from her bed uttering loud, unloving paragraphs. Oops! Wrong wife! I won't say that any wife would have reacted any differently, but hearing the plaintive, effusive apology from HB-2 prompted my bedroom-partner to call out into the darkness, "For goodness' sake, would someone please shut the wall?" Hilarity all around! This sort of crazy activity continued all night. Not much sleeping took place.

By the next day, not only were the hosts and hostesses sleepless and sooty, but the men were suffering from what is commonly called a hangover. The Saint was still in the wheelbarrow, and we contemplated leaving him there. I saw HB-2 and HB-3 make a miraculous recovery. We propped them against the posts when the guests began to arrive. With glassy eyes, they remained there for a while, but before long, their eyes began to glimmer with life, and then they were part of the gang again. They attributed this recovery to milk punch! HB-4, a.k.a. Shiftless, was well rested and ready for the day.

Well, the party was a great one. The men started a tournament of half-rubber; we shot some skeet, played horseshoes and gave tractor rides to the kiddies. The children, who must have numbered in the thousands, had tremendous fun with only minor mishaps. And best of all, since many of the multitude invited also brought their own dogs along to have a romp in the country, we had only seven dogfights. This may be a record. (It is a funny thing how people felt they had to bring their dogs along with them when invited out to Limerick.) All in all, the party was a huge success.

While rehashing (bad pun) the party—by the way, we had to do away with The Saint's hash with an A-minus for effort, but F-minus for content—we decided that the barbecue had indeed been as real as possible. We were still alive, and there was not a morsel of anything left, a sure sign of perfect planning.

Oh, yes, there was one thing left. We found a cake, mysteriously hidden under a bed. The Saint, though somewhat abashed, admitted to having stashed the cake. He explained that the person who brought the cake was well-known for taking home with her what she brought, and this time, he said, he wanted a piece of that cake. Not a very saintly maneuver, but the cake was delicious, and it surely would have gone back home with its donor otherwise. While the cake was being devoured, and in our great flush of success, we made plans for a repeat performance the following year.

With that report, you will deduce that I was slated to raise pigs on my patio for years to come. Oh, goody.

Half Price

L **ittle by little**, it was becoming clear to all and sundry that Limerick life definitely fit into the realm of the atypical. This realization had edged into my own thinking for some time, but the occurrence I am about to relate brings "different" to the edge of the absurd. As for any city-dweller—well; no one in his wildest imagination could invent the following afternoon at Limerick. I have a difficult time believing it myself.

It began simply enough. Elizabeth, who professed her desire to be a city-dweller at least twenty out of twenty-four hours, was the instigator of the plot triggering the disintegration of what had promised to be a fine afternoon. For reasons known only to her, she wanted to have a snake. I can only assume a harmless one.

It so happened that Richard, her little brother, was penniless at the time. The pot began to boil when Elizabeth told Richard that if he would get one, she would like to rent it. There. That was the background to the day in point. Simple enough. If this business deal should come to fruition, then both parties would be satisfied and life would be just rosy at Limerick. What a nice thought!

I was cutting grass, an occupation I found as gratifying as any in my inventory of required chores. I was enjoying myself immensely, just chugging along, back and forth, watching the neatness of the clipped lawn grow behind me. Often I have asked myself why I liked to cut grass so much, as have many of my friends who think I am loony for wanting to mow. But like it I did. It must be that this was one way to rectify my lack of neatness in other things.

So this was exactly what I was doing when, quite abruptly, my resolute thoughts on neatness were interrupted by Courtenay. She came running along beside me and asked me in a most agitated tone for a match. Since I thought it rather suspicious for any little girls to be playing with matches, I asked her why. She shouted back (the mower was making such a noise) that it was really Richard who wanted a match, and he wanted it now. Of course this did not make the request any less suspect. But the urgency in her voice compelled me, again, to ask why, this time cutting off the mower.

I was not prepared for the explanation. In her most matter-of-fact tone, she stated, "Because he has a snake by the tail," as though that were the most normal explanation in the world.

"Oh, is that all," I said, followed by "What?" as the full implications of what she had said began to sink in. Needless to say, my curiosity was aroused, especially as I tried to ascertain how a match figured into this picture. But this also had an easy explanation—or at least so it seemed to Richard and Courtenay. While still trying to comprehend the relationship between having a snake by the tail and needing a match, we reached Richard, who most assuredly had firmly in his grasp the hindmost quarter of a very long chicken snake that had been snagged as he was about to slither under the house. One glimpse of the vanishing snake had set Richard's most extraordinary mind to work:

1 | He had chickens and ducks that were fair game for this

shoulderless soul.

2 | Elizabeth wanted to rent a snake, which would . . .

3 | Fill his empty coffers with needed dough. So . . .

4 | He grabbed the snake by the tail.

Logic. Pure logic. Wouldn't anyone have done the same? Of course they would.

Now I was made privy to the explanation of needing the match. This too made perfect sense to Richard. Upon finding its progress considerably hampered, the snake had wrapped its front quarter around a pipe under the house, thereby creating this standoff at OK Corral. Neither the snake nor Richard was going to give an inch. But only Richard would have thought of matches. He reasoned that if you touched an embedded tick with an extinguished match, it supposedly, in reaction to the heat, would back out and leave you alone. (An old wives' tale of doubtful validity.) So, surely, the same principle would work on this recalcitrant chicken snake! Now, I really must admit that I do not know of anyone who has ever tried to heat up a snake for any reason, but I can tell you unequivocally, from experience, that it won't work, especially in the wind.

By now, I will confess, I was thoroughly intrigued and decided to enter the adventure. I had never touched a snake before, nor had I wanted to, but truthfully, a snake is not nearly so fearful a thing when its head is out of sight.

This was a right sizable snake, maybe an inch and a half thick, and long enough to tie himself in a double knot and still hang out quite a bit. I watched for a few minutes—even helped strike the matches, I am ashamed to say—and then decided that perhaps a grown-up needed to settle this thing once and for all. So I volunteered my services to help extricate the snake. Richard seemed pleased with that thought. He is such a nice little boy!

I took a firm grasp of the snake and pulled while Richard continued to light the matches. Nothing happened. I pulled a little harder, and it seemed to give a little. At the same time, I began to wonder what one would do with a snake in the hand if it did come out. Richard assured me this would not be a problem. So I yanked again. Yes, it definitely gave a little more. "Stand back," I said bravely. It was clear that I had no conception of what this little brigade of snake-nappers might look like to any observer. But I was not concerned with appearances. I was in this adventure full tilt now. So for the third time I pulled very hard, and success was mine. Out it came!

The release was so sudden I nearly fell backwards. When I regained my balance, the first thing I saw was Richard's face. Obviously, there was a problem. Indeed there was. It was readily apparent that only the back quarter, or maybe I should say half, of the snake had come out! The front half of the snake had stayed beneath the house, and there I was holding the back half! I thought then and there that I would throw up! Yuck! Double yuck! I had pulled a snake in two! Gross! For the sake of the children I tried to remain cool. Why I should have felt any worry concerning those two who had placed me in such a predicament, I won't ever understand. The worst part of all was the look of utter disgust on both their faces, as if to say, "How could you?" I was in complete agreement. How could I have done such a thing?

It was obvious that I had ruined everything for everyone concerned, especially the snake! The business deal of the century had been derailed. Financial ruin set in for Richard, and Elizabeth—well, she would just have to get a grip!

All I could do, in the face of all this misery, was to shrug my shoulders and suggest that perhaps Elizabeth would be willing to pay half price for half a snake! The suggestion was not well taken. Oh well, another ho-hum day at Limerick Plantation!

I went back to cutting the grass, which, as I said before, was a much more satisfying way to spend an afternoon.

Sugar

Cows! What odd creatures they are! I have always loved cows. We had one when I was growing up. Her name was Bossy, and she kept us in milk, cream and butter during the war when things were rationed. I wasn't very good at being a milkmaid, but my father encouraged me to help him milk (made me), saying it would strengthen my hands for playing the piano. Ah, now, that was a new one!

There is a certain smell about cows that I find pleasing and, of course, there are some other odors about them that are certainly the opposite, but I do like it when a cow lets you scratch her in that odd indentation in her forehead just under where the horns might be. (I don't like to scratch them if they have horns.) Though they seem to like it, it is difficult to tell, because as far as communicating with anyone goes, cows certainly don't. They just chew. All day long, they chew. I guess that is what makes them cows! Yes, they are odd creatures, but lovable old clods nevertheless. However, there were moments at Limerick when I yearned to murder them slowly, roast them on a spit, or turn them loose (on purpose) to eat someone else's garden.

The lowlands of South Carolina are an ideal range for raising cattle. Green grass is in evidence nearly eleven months out of the year, and the climate is so temperate, barns and other outbuildings are unnecessary. This suited our situation at Limerick perfectly, since there was no barn (inadvertently burned) and we lacked cross-fencing. The Earl of Limerick recognized this fact to be a fine opportunity to increase his reputation as The Farmer in the Dell, as well as a way to, perhaps, create some sort of income from our land at Limerick.

His Honor made good his vow to improve the herd. We had started with a handful of woeful-looking critters and now had as many as our acreage could support. Thanks to two fine bulls—the first a magnificent Hereford named Curly, and later a Charolais bull called Percy—our calves were first-rate, and fetched a good price at market. The bull calves were sold and the heifers were kept to reproduce. Therefore, in theory, our being in the cattle business was no-muss, no-fuss. But troublesome these cows were.

How could we ever have anticipated that letting our cows roam and constantly fertilize all of Limerick would lead to our having to police the premises vigorously because of young hippie trespassers constantly trying to collect certain kinds of mushrooms? Now, what self-respecting young mother was ever taught that cow pies could sprout hallucinogenic mushrooms? Certainly I was not, but chasing off weirdos became a serious pastime one summer. I did not want to be a party to their becoming even more weird because of a visit to Limerick. This was a very trying time!

In addition to this, I was faced with the constant wayward activity of our cows, which prompted a great need to improve my skills in the fine art of cow-chasing. You see, no matter where these cows were, there was usually a good reason why they should not be

there. Because I was at home more often than anyone else,
it fell to me to be the main chaser of cows, whether it was to
chase out or to chase in, as the case might be. It became nearly a
full-time occupation—not a very interesting one—and an entirely
frustrating one.

As a result of this hectic activity, I came to know these cows
very personally. Most had names, since the children named the
calves as soon as they were born. For example, after we acquired
the Charolais bull, our first white calf was named Casper the Ghost.
Another white calf, Honey, was born blind and was completely
ostracized by its mother and the rest of the herd. We had to
feed her by hand, on The Patio, until she grew big enough to
fend for herself.

Our most prolific mother cow was our oldest cow, one that was
already at Limerick when we came. Her name was Sugar. Being a
bit older, she was more friendly than the rest of the herd—in fact,
I would say she was our only cow that, in any way, had a
personality. Also, she had a most distinctive appearance.
Obviously not having the pure pedigree that Curly or Percy could
provide, Sugar did not have a nice white face like a purebred
Hereford. Her face was spotted and splotched with red, and every
calf she produced was marked in like fashion, making genealogical
records on Sugar and her offspring easy to keep.

Sugar kept a close watch on the house, and it was Sugar who
demonstrated persistence to the nth degree. She had a prodigious
appetite and an uncanny nose for corn, but geraniums also suited
her just fine. She always knew when I came home with a load of
chicken feed or similar foods of interest, and often I would have
a difficult time just getting out of the car without letting her in.
Visualize, if you will, a wrestling match with a large, splotch-faced,
forceful cow!

In fact, Sugar got into anything and everything. One day, we watched Sugar engineer a way to get the lid off the corn barrel, raise herself on her hind legs and balance on the rim of the barrel with her neck. She then proceeded to munch away. Just how she could swallow was hard to comprehend, but swallow she did until sated. With her annual splotch-faced calf nearby, Sugar was always hanging around looking for more.

Once, our relatively quiet Sunday dinner was rudely interrupted by the loud honking of an automobile's horn. Looking out the window, we saw no one there. In a short while, we heard it again, and still no sign of anyone about. Before long, the honking became a steady beep, beep, beep, and that had to be investigated. Sure enough, it was Sugar! True to her nose, she had known that my car, the old blue station wagon, was laden with her favorite groceries. Somehow, she had maneuvered enough to get her head through the window, and then into the back seat. With every swallow of corn, she would hit the horn, causing a steady, rhythmic honk, which caused us to laugh much too hard to finish our own meal. What a cow she was, and what an influence she exerted over her sisterhood.

During my tenure as keeper of cows, those bovine bottomless pits ate countless vegetable gardens, whole fields of corn and soybeans, and all my fruit trees, and on occasion they crossed the highway to devour some research the federal government was conducting at the Experimental Station. Sugar was known also to have eaten the cattails and sea oats that decorously filled the terra-cotta pots by the front door. I rarely could keep any hanging baskets longer than a week.

Sugar couldn't live forever, but even at the end of her long and fruitful life, things were different with her. One morning, we discovered her lying down in the woods, and she wouldn't—and couldn't—get up. This was most distressing, so we called The Vet. I wish we hadn't.

"Well, she can't just lie there," he preached. "If you can't get her

up, at least turn her over twice a day." It took me only a minute
to know that turning over a half-ton of cow was not in my realm
of capabilities. His answer to that was a suggestion that we pull
her tail and shout "boo" to scare her up. I hung up the phone
in exasperation.

Thus it fell my lot to be nurse to Sugar, who was down some
hundred yards in the woods. St. Nick would sail off with the
children into the morning fog and shout, as he pulled away, "Take
Sugar a bale of hay and some water." A bale of hay is heavy, and so
is a bucket of water, but they were necessary if I was to help Sugar.

It was my duty. So I would put on my old clothes and carry the
bucket of water to where she lay. Then I would wrestle the bale of
hay over to her and try to feed her. It was pure, tender loving care
for three days. It was also sad. She wouldn't eat, and would just look
at me with that big, splotched brown face of hers and then put her
head down. I felt totally inadequate.

I was sitting by her side, contemplating her situation, when a
most horrendous thing happened, right while I was sitting there.
I admit it may be hard to believe this, but Sugar took a drink of
water, looked at me with an aggrieved expression, and began to
blow a bubble out of her other end! It was a large bubble. I gasped
and decided that she must have developed some sort of horrible
hemorrhoid from lying down so long. I am very embarrassed at
that thought now, but don't forget, I was very inexperienced with
downed cows and rear-end bubbles. I was even more aghast when a
hoof appeared in the bubble. Somehow, but oh, so slowly, I grasped
the situation. I was about to become midwife to my fifth child! Oh,
no! What to do? I hardly knew where I got my own children!

A frantic race back to the house brought no help from any court.
No Vet. No Saint. Only Rip, the dog. So back I raced to Sugar,
who told me once again that she really wasn't up to all this. This I
already knew! Then I remembered the Experimental Station across

the road and ran over there for help. I really needed help, even if it was experimental! One of the men came with me and he, more or less, knew what to do (it was a cinch I didn't), and together we delivered Sugar's last calf. I don't know what would have happened if that man hadn't come!

Thus, Sugar Baby came into our lives and Sugar went out. Rip, our wonder retriever, cleaned off the little calf, who had Sugar's inevitable splotched face, and we stood back and watched her stand up and walk for the first time. Remember that magical scene in Bambi? Everyone should have such an awesome experience at least once in his life! It was truly a wonderful feeling to witness those first steps, but made even more so when the baby was mine!

As was customary practice, Sugar Baby was moved to The Patio, where she lived in the doghouse until she was too big to fit into it anymore. We fed her out of an obscene-looking bucket, mixing a milky concoction called, of all things, Calf O' Lait. Sugar Baby was healthy and seemed to be happy. Why shouldn't she be? In this natural order of things at Limerick, it was quite sensible for this calf to think that the big red dog was her mother! We had two golden retriever puppies at the time, and they thought the calf was *their* mother! I suppose that left me to be the grandmother.

We all lived happily ever after on The Patio. Needless to say, we suffered the usual problem of Sugar Baby always wanting to come into the living room, once getting as far as being able to steal the Easter lilies off the coffee table. But then, there wasn't anything unusual about that. Wasn't she one of us? If we could have pigs on The Patio, why not have family calves?

Burn, Baby, Burn

Flames and billowing smoke blanketed the air. Our house was literally ringed with fire. Standing on The Patio, watching it creep towards us, I found it possible to imagine what it would be like to be caught in a forest fire. Not good thoughts! But with this fire, there was an added dimension. It had been deliberately set, and I began to suspect that arson must run in our family! I shall explain.

Seriously, a fact of life in the Lowcountry is something called a controlled low burn, whereby all the underbrush in a forest is deliberately set on fire every year. This is usually done in early February, before the sap is up and before the strong spring winds come. And it is usually done on a calm night, when the dew helps to control the blaze. Consequently, at this time of year, lower South Carolina can give the appearance of having gone up in smoke. This is a timber conservation practice, and the results of such seeming madness are good, so say the foresters: Dead leaves and grass, fuel for potential forest fires, are consumed; potash is put into the soil and trees are given breathing room. All this is important in the proper management of timberlands. Or so I have been told.

For years I lived in dread and fascination as the burning time approached each January when Old Pyro and his Junior Pyro-cadets trooped out to burn. The children loved those pyrotechnic exercises and invited friends to participate. The friends loved it, too. I feel quite sure that their parents were unaware of the precise nature of these burning invitations, but a multitude of Beaters was a good thing when a burn was about to take place.

Nighttime burning was always an awesome sight, with the entire forest lit by the eerie flicker of what resembled a million torchlights. The sky would become greenish orange as the fire burned into itself, thereby creating an enormous whoosh of whirling flames reaching high into the night sky. And then it was over. The fire had "crowned"—a new-to-me part of fire lingo.

As a result of this burning, besides helping out our forests each year, the ground was left black with soot and ash and would stay so for several weeks until the first green shoots of new grass appeared. The children remained black up to the kneecaps during this period, as well. The dogs were the same. Housekeeping became a greater challenge than usual, and the smell of smoke permeated my world. This was part of the yearly work cycle at Limerick.

The main Pyro, St. Nick, was a fascinating man with a match. What style! What class! The rest of us might need two or three matches to get just a little patch of grass glowing, but Old Pyro, with one flourishing sweep of his arm, could set the world afire. A real talent! The children and I were mere neophytes in comparison. It was already apparent that Diji would also be a virtuoso. I am not sure that I got the same pleasure from burning, but I found myself in the middle of such work often—usually when a fire had escaped. When this happened, all and sundry, even Elizabeth, were pressed into service. The condition resulting from an escaped fire was referred to as a "high burn," which can harm trees, or in some cases become a wildfire, which is scary, and in extreme cases, a full-fledged forest fire can result, which . . . we won't even go there!

With such terms as "crowning," "backfires," and "the wind laying down" thrown into my brain through the years, I was taught what they all meant, I think. At least, I know that before you can begin to light up the world, certain conditions must be in effect. A low burn cannot be achieved if the wind is up, so it is important to wait for it to lay down, which is often at night.

Our Limerick history has proved that at Limerick, our schedule for burning and the wind's schedule for laying down have never been coincidental. Therefore, when the first lighted match was thrown, the wind was usually up, and in no time at all there was a potential holocaust. When this occurred, everyone stood on the ready to run wherever the need was greatest, ready to beat out anything that escaped. The battle cry was "Burn, baby, burn!" The weapons for beating were pine saplings.

I recall, vividly, one weekend, which had been chosen for the burning of Limerick even though there was a possibility the wind might get up. Having plowed around the perimeter and carefully explained the theory of backfires, Old Match was hopeful that we could get the job done before an upwind came into the picture. He then lit the grass at my feet. (Some people get the world laid at their feet. I got Dante's Inferno!) He then gleefully sauntered away, dropping matches as he went. Before leaving, he had given me, for my very own, a longleaf pine sapling. It was with this sapling that I was to beat, if the fire went where it shouldn't. By the time he reached the other side of the field, there was a prodigious wall of flames behind him, spreading at a great rate of speed. Judging the wind, which was a bit stronger now, he circumnavigated the field with his torch, the idea being that these waves of flames would burn into each other and put themselves out. This was the backfire principle. This was a correct assumption if the wind remained in one direction. However, the wind this day did not cooperate. Old Torch's saunter became a fast run, and I now knew for sure whence came the phrase "in hot pursuit"! Reaching Courtenay and me, he grabbed his own young pine tree. We all began beating in earnest, for if we did not succeed in blotting out this wall of fire, we would have a bona fide uncontrolled burn on our hands, with the house in the middle. Well, "where there is fire, there is smoke." No truer statement has ever been uttered.

How we did beat! I became Joan of Arc! I was a Salem Witch! I was at the gates of Hades! I was the Goddess of Fire! I was half-dead, and I feared I had already lost my eyebrows. No time to look. All the while I was beating, I was being counseled by the Main Pyro in a discreet roar to "beat, dammit, beat!" By the time everything was back under control, our sapling beaters were mere stalks, the needles having been shed on the battlefield of the flaming South Forty. "Whew," said Old Torch with a grimy grin. "That was close! Now let's go burn the avenue!" And he was off like a shot, flinging his matches this way and that, not hearing, or heeding, my reminder that we had invited company for supper.

Exhausted, I sat down to rest on the old plantation well, watching the developing conflagration and clutching my new pine branch. As I sat there, I couldn't help but let my thoughts stray from the fire and drift into thinking about this well. It was the well for the old house, and it was so old. The well cap was an enormous bowed piece of stone, with a worn notch in its central opening where the bucket had been let down thousands of times in days of yore. Peering down into that perfectly round cylinder of ancient brick, I saw lacy ferns and dark green moss growing out of the old bricks. In the twelve or so feet of water shimmering far below in the bottom, the image of my sooty face peered drunkenly back at me. I wondered what secrets were hidden in those dark depths.

There was bound to be something: perhaps a family treasure clutched in the arms of a Yankee or British soldier, perhaps the bones of a murderer—or a murderee, or perhaps—oh well, there was a resident ghost at Limerick, so there could be something!

I was roused from such wayward tricks of the mind by a shriek from Courtenay, who was down at the gate. Her words were unintelligible, but obviously she needed help. Dragging our trees, we all converged on the gate as fast as we could. The whole roadside was in flames. The whole quarter of a million acres of the Francis Marion National Forest could be next! That would never do. Cows were one thing, but the forest was unthinkable! Beat, beat, beat! Cough, cough, cough! Wheeze! Eyes smarting, throats clogged, we ran hither and thither with our pine boughs. At last, things were back under control except for one tree on the highway, and a single spark could get it going again. We posted a sentinel to guard it. As it got dark, all of Limerick glimmered with the results of these fiery shenanigans. There was an eerie but beautiful glow over the entire place that won't soon be forgotten. It was Magical Hell Hole Swamp.

In our energetic work, we had not even noticed that our guests had arrived. Leaving the boys in charge, I retreated to The Patio with them. My burning for that day was finished. And it was comforting to know that it would be a full year before any desire to burn would surface again at Limerick.

Duck Hunting

Hunting is a way of life in the Lowcountry, and of all the things a hunter needs, the first is a good place to hunt. Limerick provided The Saint with the nirvana of hunting places.

With true Venus vs. Mars intuition, it was my observation that hunters, especially men from the Lowcountry of South Carolina, were involved in some sort of hunting season about twelve months out of every year. It used to begin with deer season and end with quail season. Maybe it still does, but in addition, we now had to pay homage to a fifty-five-week football season, which overlapped a forty-eight-week basketball season, which practically eclipsed good old-fashioned baseball. With soccer, golf, hockey, tennis, and fishing, there was hardly any time left over for the main attraction, hunting. This overload did not seem to unsettle the patriarch, who managed to enjoy them all equally and somehow manage to make a living!

But as a direct result of his obsession with hunting and other sports, my own life became intertwined with these manly pursuits. There really was no escape. So I got used to playing second fiddle to a golden retriever. After all, I did have a freezer full of game, which I've always really loved, for the table! Personally, I would have liked it better if the frozen rabbits had not resembled the Easter bunny, but we hunter's wives learn to take the bitter with the better. And part of the bitter was not being able to join in the getting of the game, which, from the tall tales that were told, seemed to be a lot of fun. It was not that women were never allowed to hunt at Limerick. In fact, there were special occasions when we were invited to go along—primarily, I've always thought, so that we'd be impressed by the skill, acumen and determination of the sportsmen. But for most of the duck season, it was definitely a man's world.

My fellow hunting widows were vociferous in their complaints about being left at home so much, but once we came out to Limerick to live, I made a very interesting discovery. For the first time, I realized that when I was left at home for The Hunt, my home was right in the middle of The Hunt! Consequently, in the spirit of "do or die," I promoted another old adage: "If you can't lick 'em, join 'em." It occurred to me that I just might have some bargaining power for obtaining membership in what seemed to be a closed fraternity. It was worth a try.

There was, at Limerick, that which was called The Bunk House, and it contained sixteen beds for the convenience and debatable comfort of the hunters. It was off-limits to ladies. Such a place enabled The Hunting Buddies to come out to Limerick the night before a hunt, have supper, smoke, drink, play cards and immerse themselves in male bonding. As an added attraction, at three in the morning they would already be where they needed to be for the hunt. To complete any hunting visit, a big breakfast followed the morning hunt, and then the men could make their way back to the office—maybe. All this was very convenient and was a lot of fun for

them. But it added a bit of extra work for me. If only those Bunk
House walls could talk! There could easily be ten more chapters in
this weighty tome! I have witnessed the epitome of good-ol'-boyism
at The Bunk House. I have seen (or rather heard) the walls expand
and contract with the uneven rhythm of the mighty snores of
many tired (decoded as possibly inebriated) hunters, who snoozed
soundly with their shotguns clutched to their chests and their dogs
on the beds with them—dreams of duck-hunting glory obviously
dancing through their heads.

If truth were to be known, I was envious of this mysterious male
world and its base enjoyment of life. More than anything else,
I felt left out. Therefore, I proposed to Old Hunt Master that if I
was to be the one to change sixteen beds and get things in order
between hunts, then, in exchange, I should be able to join in the
hunts. It was a bargain, pure and simple. And it worked. There
were conditions, of course. I was not allowed to join in the male
bonding evenings, because, I was told, it would inhibit the men's
spontaneity. (I concluded that this involved the use of unladylike
words, not to mention the only-for-men's-ears jokes and stories
that were boisterously shared throughout such evenings.) I accepted
that stipulation, but I did wonder why it was that while I was not
allowed to enter The Bunk House, it was perfectly all right for
nine-year-old Courtenay, who was known to these men as St. Nick's
daughter Bubba, to frequent these masculine quarters at will. "She's
different," was all I was ever told. There seemed a certain finality to
those words, and I knew better than to pursue the subject.

As a result of this participation agreement, chauvinistic though it
was, I learned a great deal about the art of duck hunting, and most
of what I learned was, I have to admit, impressive. I was already
aware that keeping the old rice fields in the proper condition to
create happy hunting grounds was of prime importance. And I
knew that it was essential that the duck field shouldn't show the

slightest indication of having been disturbed between hunts. But I knew next to nothing about the rest of the process that ensured a perfect hunt.

For instance, it was imperative to be in the blinds before daylight, and this involved the logistics of stringing the decoys and either taking hunters to the blinds by boat or taking them to where they could walk to the blinds. This required a fair amount of planning, not to mention that it was time-consuming. So a morning hunt began around 4 a.m. This was gruesome, made even more so by the hunters' absolute delight in truly abominable weather conditions. It has something to do with when and how and at what height the ducks flew, but the colder, wetter, and foggier the weather, the better, it seemed, and the men thrived on those hideous conditions! I persevered, but it was not easy.

All-important, of course, was having proper hunting gear, especially waders. Often I have threatened, for the fun of it, to write a little essay on the individuality and variety of techniques used by hunters in pulling on their waders. You thought pantyhose were difficult? It was a remarkable sight to observe the gyrations of men, of all shapes and sizes, shimmying into noodly waders, each having worked out his own personal solution for pulling on the cumbersome equipment. Some waders, if the men were large, stuck to them like girdles, while others had loose ruffles around the chest as the straps held them up. Lord help anyone who fell out of a boat or lost his balance and sat down in the frozen water wearing waders!

Needless to say, in the category of having the right paraphernalia for hunting, I achieved the status of stepchild, never having bought the first article of hunting clothes. I was relegated to using the leftovers, the castoffs, things that no self-respecting hunter would ever be seen in. Nor was I given a pair of waders, which allow you to wade in often near-freezing water that's above your waist. I was, however, given some old hip boots once, which stopped just

short of my hips but had a tear in them just below the surface of
the water. Therefore, I can personally affirm that duck-hunting
water is very cold. The rest of my wardrobe followed the pattern:
no gun of my own, no proper hunting coat or hat, though I was
often privileged to wear my father-in-law's old war-surplus German
overcoat. It dragged on the ground, and I certainly didn't resemble
Rommel, but it was warm!

Next on my duck-hunting tutorial program was acquiring a
working knowledge of ornithological basics. Knowing the habits
of each type of waterfowl, and recognizing shapes and set of wings,
seemed like second nature to The Hunting Buddies. But I was
clueless, and an impressive amount of information needed to
be mastered.

Once I was accepted, I discovered that one of the first difficulties
for me was to get beyond what I call Duck Blind Banter. It was
some time before I could get this into perspective. These Hunting
Buddies were nice, churchgoing men—bankers, doctors, lawyers,
real estate magnates, and the like. They laughed and joked all
the time in The Bunk House. They relished taking their turns at
cooking supper or breakfast, and they seemed to like each other.
That is, until they reached the duck blind. Then, how they spoke
to one another was appalling. I couldn't believe my ears. The names
they called each other were nothing short of abusive. How they
yelled at one another! The Saint explained, as best he could, that
this was just the way it was—a man thing—and it meant nothing
personal. But I winced every time someone was cursed for not
having his hat on right, or missing a shot, or, God forbid, shooting
too soon or not at all. No one was immune.

After I had agreed to abide by the duck hunter's code, my
tutorial program began. When I was a youngster, I was a pretty fair
shot with a .22 rifle, but I had never fired a shotgun. Therefore,
shotgun lessons were my first step in joining the hunters.

The second step was trying to be a good sport while being taught by Old Fuss and Feathers. Chivalry was completely dead in the duck blind!

In those days, on those rare occasions when wives went along on a hunt, husbands, any husbands, in any duck blind, where silence was the rule, had perfected the art of regularly raising their voices at their spouses while speaking under their breath—like a raspy whisper, don't you see. It was a clever trick, and caused all conversations to take on a rather menacing tone. This was very effective in undermining the confidence of a wife. In the beginning of my hunting education, I just quivered and quaked, afraid to move. It was a fact that this hoarse barking contributed to my being taken advantage of on many occasions. For instance, never to carry a loaded gun was a major rule of any kind of hunting. I was all for that, but I needed lessons in how to load the gun in the first place. I can remember many occasions when Old Spouse was too busy shooting to ever help his wife learn to load her gun, by which time the ducks had already flown the coop.

Rule number two was: Never show your face to the sky. It was about this rule that most of the silent yelling was done. "The smallest movement can scare away a flight of ducks," I was told. Over and over I was reminded to "pull my hat down," or "don't look up except out of the corner of your eye," which I thought had overtones of Bunker Hill in its admonition. Or I was instructed to put a bush between myself and the heavens so the brightness of my face wouldn't show. Mainly, it was short and sweet: "Keep down, dammit, keep down!" (I suppose that was better than being called Chicken Head or Ape Butt!) Though I was anxious to learn, I got more than a little upset when my teacher kept pushing my head lower and lower until I couldn't see anything at all, while he was narrating the progress of the flights of ducks in tense, hoarse whispers. On numerous occasions, I found myself studying the tops of my boots while Old Spouse was booming away with his gun. By the time I got myself together, the ducks were gone, or shot, and I was still trying to keep my head down. Not fair.

After a couple of hunts, I had this all figured out and was determined to have a try at the ducks myself. Who has ever forgotten the first duck he ever felled? Defying Old Tutor, I raised my face to the heavens, as well as my gun, pulled the trigger, and to my utter amazement, dropped a ring-neck! At the same time, Old Grump fired and knocked one down as well. He turned to me, beaming, and had the nerve to say, "Did you see that? I got two with one shot!" Can you believe it? I have since learned that this can happen, but this was not the case on that day. I felt like leveling my own gun at my teacher. Now that would invite true chastisement!

Finally, the most important rule of the hunting scene at Limerick was that once put in place, no one was ever allowed to leave a blind, for any reason, until Old Fuss and Feathers gave the word. In other words, you were there for the duration, no matter what, and I do mean no matter what. (That is probably why this sport continues to be a man thing.)

It is well known that some people change personalities when they get behind the wheel of a fast car. Well, it was possible to see a similar thing happen to St. Nick when he got in a duck blind. Sometimes, I found it more amusing to forget all about hunting and just watch him in action. Actually, I believe he thought he was in action, at war, in a foxhole, with shells falling all around him. He crouched down with his gun poised, a scene from an old war movie. From his lips came a running account of every bird's movements, all uttered in a low monotone. As though following an RAF dogfight over the skies of World War II Britain, the monotone narration went something like this:

"Look high at eleven o'clock . . . two flights . . . look at
'em come . . . don't look up . . . here they come . . . on the
first pass, don't shoot . . . man, look at 'em . . . wait until
they get in range . . . hey, darlin' . . . look at that . . . here
they come . . . down . . . down . . . down . . . good darlin'
. . . steady . . . steady . . . don't look up . . . I said, DON'T
LOOK UP . . . Get ready . . . ready . . . ready . . . NOW!"

And up he jumps and fires away. After a lifetime of hunting,
he still gets that excited about a duck hunt. I must explain that
the "darlin'" referred to was the retriever in the blind with us, who
never got yelled at, just patted a lot. Forget all the disparaging
remarks about leading a dog's life, especially in a duck blind.

Speaking of dogs, that subject should be a special chapter in
any saga involving duck hunting. From what I have heard and
overheard, a man's reputation in the world at large, not just in the
hunting fields, is based on the worthiness of his dog's retrieving
prowess. After all, Dog is Man's best friend, is he not? Well, a
common Lowcountry belief is that there is no duck hunter worth
anything if he doesn't have a competent retriever.

I was always proud, and secretly thankful, that our Rip (and later
Bobo) was known to be the best retriever on the river! At least our
reputation stood on a firm foundation in one area and we could
hold our heads up among hunters. Rip was a golden retriever, but
hunters also prized black Labs, yellow Labs, springer spaniels and
even the little dog called a Boykin spaniel, which, by the way, was
designated the state dog of South Carolina, specially bred for this
sort of hunting. All were represented in the roster of reputation-
making animals. Usually, there were some of each breed at every
Limerick hunt.

In preparation for a life of making their masters look good, some
dogs were sent off to school. Some were lovingly trained at home,

but a constant was that these dogs, like their masters, also loved to freeze to death before dawn in pursuit of this incredible sport. I loved to sit in my cold little corner on the bank and just watch the dogs at work—or rather the men working the dogs.

I remember one dog in particular who was a very pretty golden. She loved her master inordinately but just couldn't seem to get the hang of the retrieval process. It was so funny. Her Master, who was a fine shot, always bagged his limit with little effort, but getting this dog to bring them to him was not only an embarrassing trial, but by necessity a public one at that. Everyone in the duck ponds could hear her Master give the command, "Fetch, Goldie. Fetch!" Nothing would happen. The order was given once more. Nothing but an adoring gaze at her Master was forthcoming. Then a rock was thrown to where the duck lay in the water. (He had to bring those rocks to the blind along with the rest of his heavy gear.) "Fetch, Goldie. Fetch," was heard again, as he pointed right at the bird. Again, no fetching transpired. Another rock was thrown. This would go on and on. Finally, the Master would leave his blind and wade over to the bird, and Goldie would follow along obediently. "Now, fetch, Goldie. Fetch," echoed the command. There may have been some other words thrown in to emphasize the plea, but I couldn't be sure. When nothing happened after she had been led directly to the bird, the Master would finally pick up the duck, put it in Goldie's mouth and say, "Good girl, Goldie, good girl." Unbelievable Duck Blind Banter followed every such incident. Well, pride goeth before a fall, they say, and the other hunters watching this scene from their blinds should take note of that fact. Or: "There but for the grace of God goest thou . . ."

Recognizing that the social side of the sporting world was important too, for a number of years during duck season we would have a big hunting house party, with friends from the upper part of the state and also from Charleston who would come to Limerick for a weekend of the sporting life. This sort of thing has been going on for centuries in merry old England, and I have loved reading novels where the descriptions of such parties thrilled me with envy. Our Limerick weekend frolics were far from those romantic shoots of Edwardian England. However, we did have a jolly good time during our sporting weekends. Since those parties involved all the wives, it helped allay the persistent barrage of caustic comments sent by the hunting widows to their hunter-spouses throughout the season.

On those weekends, both the main house and The Bunk House were pressed into service. I loved those weekends with their cocktails and huge dinners and merry times. Great hunt breakfasts followed the hunts, perfect for thawing out in front of the fire and regaling one another with stories of the morning's shoot. We Charleston women, all in the same boat as far as hunting equipment went, suffered a further bit of angst on these weekends, which we had not anticipated. First of all, while we were in our makeshift outfits, the wives from upstate arrived with complete sporting outfits, including waders, fur-lined hats and battery-heated socks. All in all, they appeared to have stepped from page thirty-nine of the L.L. Bean catalogue! Then, if looking fine weren't challenge enough, these upstate ladies owned their own guns! We were struck dumb with admiration. They also had learned how to take their guns apart and, even more remarkable, put them back together again. As it turned out, they could also hit any target that flew by them. We locals considered not going at all. However, realizing we would miss all the fun, we always went and continued the fun, year after year. Anticipation of the weekends heightened as we waited to see what new pieces of equipment would come with those well-turned-out Carolinians. Meanwhile, we Lowcountry ladies made our own contributions. One invention of note was a roll of toilet paper soaked in kerosene and stuffed into a coffee can, guaranteed, when lit, to heat any duck blind! I have often wondered what they, the well-equipped northern ladies, thought of us.

Eventually, I became a somewhat seasoned hunter. After many years of the above I was finally allowed to shoot in a blind by myself. The only advantage to this was that anything I hit could be claimed by me alone. Otherwise, I found it a bit lonesome. I was still noncompliant about keeping down and shooting at ducks out of range, and I was still always frozen and wet. But duck hunting is a way of life down here, and I have grown attached to that way of life.

Although my abilities were somewhat imperfect, I came to agree with the men that there was nothing so beautiful to watch as a flight of ducks, circling and circling and finally setting their wings to glide in. I counted myself very lucky to have been able to join 'em. It more than made up for my having to change sixteen beds every week! Well, almost.

Old Blue

Even before Limerick, I had gained a reputation for making do with hand-me-down modes of transportation. My cars, like the hunting clothes, were castoffs from a more important somebody, and they performed as such. I know I spent many an hour on various roadsides fixing flat tires, and many more hours at the mechanic's shop. I believe I could write an entire encyclopedia on the flats-with no-workable-spares that I have had to endure. However, generally speaking, my vehicles got me where I needed to go.

But once upon a time, I acquired a brand-new automobile, the first I had ever been given for my very own. It was a new Dodge Dart, the premier and only—as far as I know—push-button car ever produced. I was intrigued with the idea of pushing buttons to shift gears. It seemed a fine and dandy idea. And, for a short time, it was. However, I soon was faced with buttons that came loose upon application of a fingertip, and often they would slip sideways —or, sometimes, fall to the floor! This began to occur with such regularity that I had to make it a practice always to have a Phillips screwdriver on my person in order to get wherever I wished to go. It was not unusual that I found it necessary to unscrew the entire dashboard, refit all of the buttons, then screw back the dashboard and hope that I had not mixed up forward and reverse! Perhaps this was the reason Darts were made for such a short time. At any rate, I was glad to move on to Limerick, where a new set of transportation standards awaited me in the guise of Old Blue.

I have made mention of the old blue station wagon and its role in our unconventional life at Limerick, so it is meet and right that Old Blue should have its own place in my story. When the lovely powder-blue Chevy wagon came my way, as a legacy from my Sainted mother-in-law, it was a great day for celebration. My mother-in-law never had to do what I needed to do with that car, so this fine blue vehicle came to me at a relatively young age and in very good health. I could not have been more pleased.

If cars could claim personalities, then this one was a doozy. She was an extremely good sport when put to the task of doing all she was asked to do as a heavy hauler, starting with the children and moving on to live animals, hay, fertilizer, and seeds. Old Blue could be loaded to the gills and still pull a trailer, and all the while she never gave me a moment's trouble. I was elated to have Old Blue for my very own.

In one of her lighter moments, Old Blue brought home the bacon, so to speak, when The Saint loaded it with two large boxes of butchered veal from one of our own bull calves. The meat was neatly wrapped and labeled, ready for the freezer. Unfortunately, it was one of Courtenay's favorite calves that had been sacrificed to supply this meat. So, as The Saint hefted the boxes into the kitchen, I whispered to him not to elaborate on where the meat came from. Not to worry, however. As I was separating the packages to go into the freezer, Courtenay came into the room, took one look, and went straight to the other large box. Surveying the situation at hand, she then threw her arms around the box, as best her little arms could reach, and exclaimed, "Oh, Bully, we loved you so!" Well, that did it! None of us could ever bring ourselves to enjoy Bully, eventually giving most of him away!

As the years went by, Old Blue lost most of her good looks, sagging here and there, dented and scraped from hard use, and sprouted such a carpet of rye grass in the way-back that a friend of Diji's was moved to make the comment, "Gee, I'm not getting in the back seat, I think I'm in the back yard!" Yes, Old Blue was a very good sport.

When not hauling, Old Blue was used to do field work along with the ancient truck, which wasn't long from complete retirement. In particular, she became very handy for roundup time with the cows. The Saint had much schooling on cattle-raising by now, and one lesson was that each cow should have a numbered identification tag attached to its ear, proving vaccinations of various sorts. He also had pertinent conversations with The Vet and had learned to do dreadful things to the bull calves. Both of these processes involved rounding up the cattle. When the day arrived, the words "git along, little dogie" took on some added meaning, and all children, and any friends who might be visiting, became involved in the Limerick Rodeo.

Roundup was best done with the blue station wagon. A driver was needed, usually Courtenay or The Saint. The others, all of them, were the wranglers. You could hear the "yee-ha's" echoing through the fields as these unlikely cowboys would leap from the hood or the back of the station wagon onto a fleeing bovine, and then all would join in the calf-tackling so Saint Vet could administer whatever treatment was needed at the moment. This was one operation that I had nothing to do with, reserving myself for cow-chasing of another kind, I suppose. It was not surprising that this kind of duty did nothing positive for the looks or condition of an automobile—in fact, by now, I doubt that "automobile" was an applicable term for poor Old Blue.

In the absence of the old truck, Old Blue became the chief farm vehicle, carrying boards down to The Point, dragging fallen logs to the brush pile, unsticking The Saint from whatever quagmire he was in, and even taking Wilbur off to be customized. I remember one excursion when Courtenay and I drove the entire circumference of all the rice fields, looking for something or another that seemed very important at the time. We stopped at several places, and then returned to The Bunk House to pick up the bedding that needed to be laundered. When we returned to The Bunk House, I got out and Courtenay said, "Hey, Mom! Look. The back window is gone." I turned to look and sure enough, the entire long back window on the right side was missing. We jumped back in the car and retraced our route clear around the rice fields. To this day, that window has never been located! Swallowed up by the blackberry bushes or stolen by trolls, the window was no more, and, pretty much, that marked the end of any road travel off Limerick for that vehicle. Vanity had already risen in Elizabeth, who had vowed not be seen in public in the blue station wagon, but now it was assured that Old Blue would stay home, and a brand-new white Ford station wagon would take her place.

In the meantime, Old Blue still ran like a top, but her appearance had totally disintegrated: lopsided, faded, sagging, and worn. (Sounds like a self-portrait!) How many times had she been stuck in the mud? How many cows had she caught? How many tons of so many things had she carried? How long could she go on?

Recognizing that the days were numbered for Old Blue, The Saint came bounding in exuberantly one afternoon, fresh from a great dove shoot in the upper field. "Come on," he shouted, as he pulled me away from the kitchen sink. "Want to do something you've always wanted to do, but couldn't?" He was waving his shotgun excitedly. Realizing that this was a command performance, I mumbled, "Sure," and followed him outside. Old Blue was parked just outside, and her faded glory gleamed in the late afternoon sun.

"What are you up to?" I queried, as I noted the glint in his eyes. They were positively twinkling with excitement. With that, The Saint metamorphosed into Old Scarface, Al Capone. Raising his shotgun as though it were a Tommy gun fresh from its violin case, he took aim, and peppered the car from front to back and back to front, whooping with hilarity. Ratatat! Ratatat! He sprayed the car once more. Old Blue now looked as though she had belonged to Bonnie and Clyde. The children were rolling in the grass. Their father was a lunatic!

Well, it didn't stop Old Blue or us. She went on until the bitter end—and we were used to living with lunacy. I now had acquired that larger, new, white Ford station wagon, of which we were all very proud. But, as fate would have it, in no more than one week, while we were enjoying a party at the Wando River, a freak storm blew up and felled a tree right on my new white buggy. We were off to a good start! But that too is another story.

Peter Rabbit

should have recognized we were in for another adventure when
I discovered that Richard had yet another plan. Sometimes he
disclosed his plans and sometimes he did not, but whenever
we suspected even a hint of something being afoot, it was time
to pay close attention. Courtenay's birthday was coming up, and
most assuredly, this spurred Richard's brain into motion. Richard
and Courtenay were great pals even though they were five years
apart, and it came to light during one of their many conversations
that Courtenay certainly would like to have a rabbit. That was all
Richard needed to turn his ever-fertile mind toward a new goal.
He began immediately to put his plan of acquiring a rabbit as a
birthday present for Courtenay into action. Since he was penniless,
he thought the most logical move was to trap a wild rabbit. Most
would agree that this was logical thinking for Richard.

We saw rabbits at Limerick on occasion, but we were not really
known as rabbit country, so the task of rabbit-catching was no
easy one, something Richard was soon to find out. He pressed the

two box-traps we owned into service, depositing them in what he was sure were perfect rabbit hangouts. This was early in May and the birthday was in June, so he assumed he'd have plenty of time. Since he made Courtenay help carry the traps and set them up, the trapping was no secret. But what he was trapping was hidden in much mystery, whispering and knowing looks, which were passed around liberally. Richard was blessed with enormous, very expressive brown eyes, and when they rolled or winked, everyone was aware of them.

Every afternoon, the traps were checked and rebaited, without much success as far as rabbits went. However, he did catch one coon, two possums, three rats, and two water moccasins, which made checking the traps ever an exciting experience. But still, there were no rabbits. .

A change of plan came about with the arrival of the *Farmer's Bulletin*. Richard had learned from his poultry proceedings that this little publication could feed his brain with all sorts of ideas for new plans. So when he read an advertisement for rabbits in the *Bulletin*, a short note to my sister, who lived in the city of the advertisement, achieved results. In a couple of weeks, a new creature came to our house, Easter Bunny type, and was given the original name of Peter Rabbit. Of course, Courtenay was thrilled at Richard's generosity and, of course, we said we were too. It was my turn to roll my eyes!

This rabbit had decidedly been someone's pet, a much-loved pet, for he was extremely tame. He feared nothing, not even other animals, ate from our hands and liked not his hutch one bit. He therefore spent most of his time hopping around the house. This, too, was typical behavior for many of our furry and feathered friends. It also became apparent in a very short time that Peter was no ordinary rabbit, or at least he seemed a bit peculiar to me. All my life I had heard jokes made about the prolific nature of rabbits, but with one lone male rabbit, I certainly had not anticipated anything related to problems along that line of thought.

There was a problem, however. Peter Rabbit had decided, quickly and without reservation, that he loved our cat. Of course, my original fear had been that the cat would eat the rabbit, but, silly me, this was not the case. It was nowhere near the case. Peter Rabbit would stalk the cat, jump on him, and the two would roll and tumble until the rabbit got just a mite too amorous. Then, with a loud spit, the cat would disengage himself and run and hide in disgust, the bunny in pursuit. We stayed in hysterics most of the time, watching the graceful red cat flee the bouncing white ball, the cat often climbing a tree in desperation. This went on every time the two met, and I must say that I have never observed this kind of rabbit behavior before or since. The poor cat became a nervous wreck. We were amused.

One afternoon, The Patio was put to its primary use: entertaining. We were visited by family friends and their children, who were best friends to our children. They had also brought along their show dog, Ethel. Ethel was a tiny Yorkshire terrier who was well-known to many in downtown Charleston. She had the heart of a lion but the body of a mouse, and Ethel had a deserved reputation for running away. In the past, many a dinner party in town had been interrupted by errant Ethel's wanderings. At these times, up and down The Battery, in the dark, could be heard heartfelt entreaties emanating in stentorian tones from her mistress:

"Ethel, come! Ethel, come!"

Ethel rarely did come. So I was surprised that Ethel was allowed to visit Limerick, a place so wild and mysterious to a tiny little mutt like Ethel. But there she was, sitting on her mistress's lap, nicely brushed and sporting a new blue ribbon in her hair. She was a perfect lady, in spite of being completely overwhelmed by the arrival of several cows at the edge of The Patio. It was obvious that Ethel had never met a cow before. She was beside herself with excitement, and we laughed and laughed at her antics.

Well, as the afternoon progressed, we were having a libation on The Patio, watching the children have a good time, completely absorbed in rollicking good conversation, when the cow situation took a dim back seat to the events at hand.

Peter Rabbit bounced out to say hello, the cat keeping an eye on the entire proceedings from the heights atop the doghouse. This solitary event was to erupt into one of the funniest sights in my memory. In no time at all, it became very obvious that Peter Rabbit took one look at beautiful Ethel, with her lovely blue bow, and threw over his great love, the cat. It was true. Peter experienced the lightning-bolt shock of Love at First Sight.

There was a flurry of white and gray at our feet as Peter pressed his ardor on poor, unsuspecting, tiny Ethel. With a hysterical yip, Ethel leaped off The Patio and, cows or no, went bounding frantically down the hillside towards the rice fields. The familiar call, "Ethel, come!" resounded across the land. But it was to no avail. Down through the tall weeds went Ethel, with Peter Rabbit right on her coattails. Like the proverbial bouncing white ball, Peter bounded after her—almost quite literally into the sunset. We were all consumed with laughter as the incessant "Ethel, come!" echoed over the rice fields. Poor Ethel could not climb a tree as the cat could, and by the time she was retrieved, her hair was a mess, dripping with marsh grass, and her blue bow was definitely missing. While I am quite sure her honor was intact, there was no getting around the fact that Ethel was embarrassed. We were exhausted from laughing so hard. The cat was elated! Peter was disappointed. What a day!

Sadly, this unusual amusement, Peter Rabbit, was with us for only a short time. One day, Peter Rabbit woke up dead. We didn't know why, and we feared to tell Courtenay that her beloved though madcap pet had gone on to his great reward. Forgetting how tough and resilient youngsters can be, we observed that she was very matter-of-fact about the whole thing. It was not long before we learned that plans for an elaborate funeral ceremony were nearly completed. There was much digging and making of a cross, and preparations for a procession were in place. I was relieved they didn't want me to play the organ, though I was invited to attend.

When all was prepared, out marched a cortege composed of our four children, plus the five from across the road, and a string of puppies. All were singing something that sounded a great deal like "Yo, Heave Ho," but it didn't seem to matter that the tune brought a different kind of work to mind. Coming last in the procession was Courtenay, bearing her beloved Peter Rabbit aloft. Courtenay never walked, she strode, and Peter was not ceremoniously laid out in a box, or wrapped carefully, but triumphantly held high, like a torch. For, you see, by now old Peter was stiff as a board, and Courtenay must have felt that this was the correct way to send him to the great Hereafter. And I am quite sure that Peter did go to his great reward. His short tenure at Limerick was appreciated by all of us.

Whatever would the world be without children?

Vacation

Once upon a time, and only once, this family went on a vacation trip. I say once, because it really was a one-time happening, never before and never again. It wasn't that The Saint did not get a vacation, but it had been our usual practice to take his vacation time during duck season so that Big Dad could squeeze the trigger a few times and keep himself in a proper frame of mind for work and life in general. Since we always went to Limerick, which we all loved, and now we lived there, no one ever complained. We loved it. Limerick was a vacation!

Consequently, we were amazed one day when Dad announced that we were going to the Outer Banks of North Carolina for the Fourth of July. At this point, our knowledge of the Outer Banks was limited, but we leaped with joy at the thought of a family trip. None of us was aware that he had arranged to borrow a motorized camper in which to make the trip. He got it from the same place that had supplied The Bulldozer. It was clearly going to be an adventure. This was on Thursday evening. We were to leave on

Friday, the very next day! Nothing like giving any notice!

Old Travel Planner had done his homework, and we were
informed that the only way to get to the Outer Banks—and
Okracoke Island, in particular—was by ferry. Just think of it, a
recreational vehicle and a ferry. Too much! I was beginning to
feel worldly.

Obviously, haste was the operative word. In order to ensure
our getting to Okracoke before nightfall, it was necessary to board
the ferry in the wee hours of the morning. Visions of spending
our entire vacation waiting for a ferry spurred us to gather things
together as quickly as possible. Missing a ferry would be right up
our alley.

We left after work in something of a frenzy. Quite frankly, frenzy
was our usual modus operandi, but a lot had to be done in a short
time to pull us together. Eventually, we were on our way with three
of the four children, plus Rip, our Golden Oldie, along with our
red cat, whom The Saint despised. We packed at least fourteen bags
of groceries, linens, fishing poles, crab lines and laundry I hadn't
had time to fold. We were well on the way when we realized we had
left the bicycles. Just as well, I thought. We traveled as fast as the
Winnebago could take us towards a vacation to end all vacations.
We were very excited as we explored the camper and put things
away while speeding down the road. Yes, it was the beginning of
a real adventure!

There was a system to the ferrying process. In order to get on the
first ferry in the morning, people parked right in line to board in
whatever vehicle they were driving. Although we drove as if we were
in a race to get into this ferry line, we were so late that we only had
to spend half the night in line! We came to a halt right behind forty
other camper-mobiles who were working under the same premise.
There were sleeping bodies draped everywhere we looked—on
hoods of cars, under bushes, in backs of trucks—quite a sight.

After our hectic departure, I felt as though I should be draped somewhere too, but I didn't yet know where. I soon found that it was my luck to be given the bunk over the driver's seat, which could only be reached by a bit of climbing. Here I was to await the sunrise and the eventual loading of the ferry. The rest of our bunch lay on various bunks and benches. I instantly discovered that my bunk was designed for pygmies. If any sort other than a pygmy tried to roll over, it was probable he or she might be wedged there forever. I vowed to remain on my back, and just knew that sleep would elude me. But doze I did, and I even must have slept, because the next thing I knew, the motor was humming. We were about to board the ferry. From where I was pinioned, it looked as though the entire world had just awakened and hadn't had time to shave! Bleary-eyed, blanket-clutching specters were milling about, and we had begun to lurch forward. Not wanting to miss any part of this ferry-riding experience, I began to descend from my perch.

Little did I know how challenging that would be. In this camper there was no little ladder by which to reach the cramped heights where I lay. In fact, the method followed for ingress and egress was a rather complicated one: right foot on floor, raise left leg to shoulder height, step on edge of sink, adroitly haul right leg up to the back of the front passenger seat and, with both legs dangling, heave torso onto bunk, hoping legs would follow. Though ungainly, it worked, and the procedure had to be reversed for getting down. This I was doing when we began to move onto the ferry. However, I missed the foot on the sink and came hurtling through the air, landing in a heap in the stairwell. Had we not locked the door, I would have rolled right out for the world to witness. As it was, two large bumps were raised where they could not be seen and at least five where they could. I was going to have a black eye for sure. The children were alarmed, and the cat spat at Dad, which further cemented their relationship. At least I wasn't dead. Still, we'd made it onto the first ferry. Mission accomplished. Soon we had a cup of coffee, which usually had a way of making things look better. I just wished I didn't hurt all over.

None of us had ever seen a body of water like the Albemarle Sound, and I must say it was impressive, but different from the seascapes we were accustomed to. Also, we discovered that there was great camaraderie among ferry riders, making the two hours it took to cross the sound a lot of fun. The only other boat on this vast piece of water was the other ferry taking other travelers back to the mainland. Soon, we sighted the lighthouse and pulled into the marina at Okracoke Island. We had made it.

The marina was aptly named: It was called Silver Lake, and it was beautiful—circular in shape, with gorgeous yachts tied up everywhere we looked. We were mightily impressed. Also, everywhere we looked there were literally thousands of people! Right away it became apparent that there was no room in any inn on Okracoke for us. At 8:30 in the morning, all the campgrounds were wall-to-wall campers and there was a law prohibiting any stopping along the road. Our camper was self-sustaining, with no need to hook up to anything, but even so, we could find no place to park our bus. Our Big Dad was a hard one to deter, so he set about finding a place to rest our bones. In spite of any and everything, succeed he did! On his search for a home, he met a local family who just happened to own a plot of ground right on the edge of Silver Lake! They let us stay there for two dollars a night, and we rented bicycles from them as well. I couldn't believe it. All the other holiday-makers were crammed into campgrounds, with barely enough room to open their doors all the way, and we were luxuriating on the edge of Silver Lake with elegant yachts as neighbors! No one should ever underestimate the powers of Big Dad. The only slight difficulty encountered was learning to live at a forty-five-degree tilt towards the water. One copes with things like that as one must. It was workable. We were having fun.

Since we had no prior experience in family vacations, we each had different ideas about what was done on such a venture. The ideas were diverse as the people. Elizabeth envisioned lying on the beach. Courtenay wanted to swim, although not in the marina but in the ocean. Richard got lost immediately while trying to figure out what he wanted to do. I wanted to see the sights our fellow ferry-riders had talked about. But Big Dad had his idea, too: We were to fall to and catch dinner! And, of course, that is precisely what we did.

Out came the crab lines and bait and the fishing poles, and we were put to work. It wasn't really work to go fishing, but it became more complicated when Dad found an old crab trap buried in the sand, and insisted we dig it up so we could catch lots of crabs at one time. We did all that, caught a nice number of fish and lots of crabs, got our first taste of hot July sun, and planned an incredibly edible menu of fruits de la mer, caught with our own hands. This menu included boiled crabs, fried fish and hush puppies, French-fried tomatoes (a new invention that Old Chef wanted to try), fried potatoes and the shrimp we had not used for bait. It sounded delicious.

We got the fire going outside, brought out the iron pot, and got the oil nice and hot, thus beginning the great gastronomic endeavor that was to be our supper. Since most of this dinner was to be prepared in the same pot, this was a do-it-in-shifts deal.

First, we boiled the crabs to enjoy while the rest of the main courses were being cooked. Nothing can surpass the taste of a sweet Atlantic blue crab! One by one, the other culinary components were cooked and sent in to the dining table where all else was waiting. The first hint of catastrophe occurred when Richard stumbled with the plate of freshly fried fish, dumping all into the sand. Bad word! We brushed them off as well as we could, just in

time to witness Courtenay coming in with the potatoes.
Finding the plate too hot, she dropped them into the sand! Two
bad words! Potatoes are pretty hard to revive after such treatment,
so we moved on to the new invention, which Dad decided to carry.
All was fine until he reached the table. As though an invisible hand
had reached out and grabbed it, the dish of French-fried tomatoes
flew out of his hand, not into the sand but against the wall, behind
the cushions and into my lap! Three bad words, and we all had a
bologna sandwich!

So went our first day of vacation, which some may think was
full of ominous portent. We all knew it was just a natural course of
events for us, and we were looking forward to the next day.

Well, the next day was simply gorgeous. To take advantage of
it, we decided to move the bus to the beach. I had been told of the
wild horses on Okracoke, and of the numerous shipwrecks along
the beaches, so I was anxious to go exploring. Elizabeth was more
than anxious to bask in the sun and the others wanted to play in
the waves, which were huge. But Big Dad had other plans for us.
We were to catch lunch! I gather that when he was a boy on the
golden sands of Florida's beaches, it was deemed quite worthwhile
to partake of delicious coquina soup. We didn't know what
coquinas were, nor did we really care, but that fact left us wide
open for a lesson in retrieving coquinas. This took the better part of
the morning, with all of us groveling around in the surf searching
for coquinas, which undoubtedly, to hear Old Saint rave, must be
the nectar of the gods. (He probably walked two miles through the
snow, barefoot, to get to school, too.) Usually we found only two
or three coquinas at a time, so getting enough for a family of five
consumed some time. Once they were obtained, the soup had to be
cooked. Evidently, the recipe for this delicacy was lost in the passing
of The Saint's years, because I wouldn't recommend coquina soup
to my worst enemy! The result of this strenuous morning tasted like

rock consommé, made with boiled, tasteless, and sandy shells. We resorted to bologna sandwiches once again.

By now, we were confronted with the problem of cramming five extremely sunburned people and a dog and cat, both full of sand, in an already too-crowded camper. On the entire trip, I don't believe we ever successfully conquered that problem, and secretly, I wonder if any campers ever do. Back at our forty-five-degree slant, the shower water ran out the door, which wasn't too dreadful because we had only enough water for one shower. What was bad was when the runaway water ran into the basket of clean clothes. Ah, the glories of camper living!

As for the island of Okracoke, it was just as quaint as we had been told, with its picket fences, family cemeteries in the back yards of weathered cottages, fishing nets hanging to dry, and windswept coastal trees. I couldn't help but feel that the natives should be terribly restless with the influx of thousands of holiday seekers, of which we were only a small part. Their lives must have been considerably more tolerable before the invention of camper-mobiles, now called RVs by the more hip crowds.

Thus far, we had eaten little more than bologna sandwiches, so it was agreed that the next night would find us having dinner at The Inn, which was renowned over the island as *the* place to eat. We rode our rented bikes over, made the reservations, and then went back to our home on Silver Lake to relax. This was done while watching Rip chase a merganser until I thought both would drown. No matter how hard Rip swam, the duck was always just out of reach, but neither would give up.

When it was time to go to dinner, we got ourselves as ready as half-washed, charred people could, and rode bikes over to The Inn. I tried to disguise my black eye with makeup. It was dusk, and the scene was very lovely. The Inn itself was totally picturesque, with driftwood in just the right places, nice watercolors on the walls and other memorabilia of the sea scattered around artistically.

I wondered why so many people were leaving. Since everything closed early on Okracoke, I dismissed the thought. I shouldn't have. We then learned that the power had been off on the island for some two hours and The Inn was completely unable to prepare a thing. Really. They were not serving one thing! By this time, we were out of bologna, so we dragged back to the camper for a scrambled egg supper. We were too bone-weary to fret much. I vowed to stock up on something more substantial the next day.

In the morning, we moved up the island and across, on another ferry, to Cape Hatteras, "Hattras" to the locals. To prove how stalwart we were in the face of starvation, we climbed the famous Hatteras Lighthouse to view the cape from on high. At that point, Mom was nearly a dropout, but eventually I did make it to the top. From there, it could plainly be seen just why this area was known as the Graveyard of the Atlantic. The cape projected far out into the sea, its shallow waters hiding the precarious shoreline so unwary ships could, and did, easily run aground.

It was also a twentieth-century scene below. At least 500 surfers were beneath us in pursuit of the enormous (in comparison to ours at home) waves.

I doubted my ability to climb back down the many hundred steps of the lighthouse, and suggested they just go on and leave me. There was more room there than in the camper anyway! But Big Dad lured me down with a promise of a good dinner at Nag's Head. Again, he was a man of his word. We had survived another day, and we did finally have a delicious dinner. All were in agreement that this was a good thing.

The next day we finished doing most of what you are supposed to do while on the Outer Banks, paid homage to Orville and Wilbur Wright, and then began the long trek home. By now, the cat had decided that Dad was his own true friend, and had taken up residence on the dashboard in front of the steering wheel. I knew this was going to cause friction, but the kitty could not be swayed, and Old Dad was a good sport about it. Or rather, he was silent about it.

We sped down the highway towards Mattemuskeet, a famous game refuge in North Carolina. Seeing this place had been a goal of all the hunters in our family for a long time, so we drove in to give it a once-over. Frankly, I was disappointed. We had a bigger lake at Limerick, and the Lodge was very ordinary. We lurched around the grounds until we found a nice little creek where we decided to fish for a while. It gave us a nice chance to catch our breath, but that was all, so we started on our way once more, fishless. Just as we were leaving, we met a person, the first and only, who informed us that this was not, in fact, Mattemuskeet. The lake was further down the highway. It was nice not to have the Mattemuskeet dreams shattered. When we finally came to the Big Lake, it was indeed enormous, and we were sorry it was not the time of year to see geese.

Now that the real lake had been viewed, we could make tracks for home. This became difficult when the cat began to throw some sort of tantrum, so much so that we had to stop and let him out. He wouldn't go out! Then we realized why. He, of all of us, was the only one who had realized that the large bag of dirty laundry we had been stepping over was not Rip, our golden retriever. Rip was gone, most probably left some thirty miles behind us, where we had gone fishing. The gloom that settled over our little band of holiday makers was gripping. Silence reigned as we turned the bus around, each one of us having his own private thoughts about Rip and what might have happened to him. None of us could voice what we thought because we all feared the worst. Surely, that was the longest thirty miles any of us ever traveled. When we reached the Lodge, luck was with us. Rip, hot and thirsty, was bounding down the road frantically looking for us. Such a reunion! How lucky we were to find him! The cat purred happily.

By now we were really behind schedule, and Big Dad steamed ahead, full throttle. We were in the coastal country of Eastern North Carolina depicted in some of my favorite historical novels. I saw several signs pointing to historic Bath, North Carolina, where the infamous Blackbeard had been captured. The tour guide in me was aroused, and I timidly broached the subject of taking the five-mile side trip into Bath. Old Chauffeur, in no uncertain terms, was not receptive to this idea. It was plain I would have to go about things in a different way. Fortunately for me, there were at least six exits to Bath. By the sixth one, I had won, but only because it was time for lunch and the driver was tired. That was all the time I needed, I assured him, as we traversed the short five miles into what we found to be a delightful little town on a wonderful cove. This was the inlet where Blackbeard, the ferocious pirate, who is always depicted with burning cigars behind his ears, took refuge on many occasions, and it was here he eventually was captured.

I was excited. I was the only one. The coerced driver couldn't see the good in anything right then, so he told me he would rest his eyes while I went to the museum. Being the good wife I was, I told him I would put on the hamburgers while he napped. Then, the race was on! I made the hamburgers and put them on, very low. The houses were scattered over three blocks, so I bought my tickets, checked the skillet, and saw the first house—quickly, mind you. I ran back to the camper, turned the hamburgers and ran to the second house, which was farther away than the first. Then I ran back, fixed the sandwiches, and told the children to give me a head start and then wake up The Driver. I would be in the third house, down by the water. They could pick me up there.

I hadn't been aware that I could run so fast, or could soak up so much history and culture at such a pace. I am quite sure the house-hostess had never given such a breathless tour, either. However, it was one I never got to complete, because the camper's horn began to blow insistently right in the middle of the trundle-bed spiel. What a time to have to go—but since prudence was the better part of valor, I flew out the door and leaped aboard the already moving camper with a driver who was glowering, not because I had gone to the museums but because I had tricked him into it. Typical male approach, and probably a typical female approach as well, but I had seen enough to satisfy me and was in a good enough mood to be properly sorry.

And I really was sorry! By now, we were so far behind schedule that when we got to the Governor's Palace in New Bern, it was closing time. After that, we steered for good old Limerick Plantation. Home! It was time, too. The Driver was tired of driving and vacations. Hunting season was really much better. The children were exhausted, and we were definitely out of bologna again.

So, with great joy and sighs of relief, we pulled into the gate at Limerick a few minutes before midnight. We all agreed that, though not very typical, we had had a wonderful time. We still had everyone we went with, and the camper would still roll. Leaning back, I enjoyed the thoughts of how nice it was to have had a vacation, just like everyone else! I couldn't wait to tell my friends all about it.

But we should have known that we couldn't return home like normal folk. As we rounded the circle, our headlights picked up the grotesque silhouettes of four very dead cows, very stiff cows, their feet poking oddly into the air under a large oak tree. Would you believe that there had been a big storm that day and these four unfortunate cows had been struck by lightning? Believe it! The problem (a big one) of what to do with dead cows would have to wait until the next day.

Ah, home sweet home! I was glad to be back, and I thought it would be best if we stuck to our old ways in the future and left vacationing to others. Life at Limerick was far more interesting!

Red!

At some point in the Limerick years, I happened to overhear a conversation that brought into focus for me how we who lived at Limerick might be perceived by others. I must admit it gave me pause.

The speaker, the husband of a cousin of one of our friends, was visiting from Georgia. To entertain these visitors, we had invited them, along with six others, out to Limerick for drinks and supper on The Patio one Sunday afternoon. They had expressed an interest in seeing Limerick, and we were always happy to see them because they were so much fun. So it was arranged. All seemed to be in order for the evening except The Patio décor. Since one of our boats had recently sunk in the fishpond, its motor was now on The Patio, where it was more convenient to study the damage. The outboard engine rested in a large galvanized garbage can. This was not exactly the plantation dinner-party atmosphere I desired to share with visitors, but I had had to put up with worse, and that was that. Be that as it may, this was the backdrop for the afternoon under discussion.

The group assembled, and the visiting Georgians were dolled up, plantation fashion, ready for a good time at our country place, as they called it. From the outset, the afternoon was destined for deterioration, but I will let the Georgian describe it as he related it to someone else a few months later. I just wish I could re-create the slow, languid, mellow South Georgia drawl in which the tale was told. It went something like this:

"Hey, have y'all evah been out to Lim'rick plant-ation? Yeah, well, suh, we were out there las' month. Is it always like that out there? I dunno, but it seemed raht strange to me. Did y'know that everything out there is ray-ud? Why, the house was red, there were red dawgs, red caows, a red pig [that was Wilbur], a red cat and some red chickens . . . and y'know, they even have red bugs! [Laughter from all.]

"They went to a lot of trouble for us, too. The table was set so pretty, and we were havin' drinks and just gettin' into tellin' some great jokes when the subject of a broken boat came up, and sure 'nough, there was a boat raht there on the patio with us. Nevah have seen a boat on a patio. I guess it was broken or something, 'cause its motor was in a garbage can full of water. Nevah have seen that before either! Well, y'know, one of the guys was a great mechanic, so it wasn't too long 'fore they went over and tried to start the motor—right there on the patio! Obviously somethin' was wrong, 'cuz a humongous cloud of black smoke poured out. It made us all cough. Then they turned it off and fiddled with somethin' . . . then turned it on again . . . then off . . . for what seemed like for-evah. I know I was having a hard time tellin' my jokes. Well, suh, the noise was awful and the fumes were too, so the rest of us had to move to the other side of the patio. But y'know what? On that side of the patio a red calf was living in a red doghouse! Now, d'ya think that's normal doin's for a suppah party? If this is the newest thing, I can't wait to try it back home.

It would be a real gasser! [More laughter]

"And then, y'know, the phone rang and rang and rang before someone could answer it. When they came back they announced what everyone but us seemed to know about. 'Well, he's out,' they said, and everyone sucked in their breath like this was really big news. I thought someone had just graduated and asked about it. 'No, no, he's just outta jail!' They said it in such a nonchalant way. I must've looked kinda funny, but all I could think to say was 'How nice!' Y'know, that's a real conversation-stopper. I don't know any people in jail. But it seemed kinda normal out there. I mean, don'cha think with caows in doghouses an' everything, jus' anything ole thing could happen?

"Well, we went on and had a real nice suppah. But, y'know, I don't think they do plantation in Jawja like they do in South C'lina."

For years after this dubious social event, I was always asked by this cute Georgian if we still served gas fumes for cocktails, or how far our boat could go in a garbage can, or something like that, and then he would go into gales of laughter. I was just glad our guests wanted to remain our friends!

Alone

Since I have already explained that cutting grass was one
of my favorite things to do, I feel I should now elaborate
on how I also loved to go fishing at Limerick. Just what
was so captivating about fishing? I think that's a question well
worth pondering.

As The Saint had become an avid angler, I had gamely put up
with the fish stories of Old Blue Fish King for some time, and I
must admit that The King's brand of fishing was too complicated
for me. I am a simple person, and I had no interest in analyzing
whether I had the right lure, or was in the right spot to catch any
particular kind of fish. I just liked to snag what ever came by in
the rice field canal, where the likelihood of seasickness was remote!
Courtenay and I liked to fish our rice field canals, and we preferred
to use cane poles and worms. Sometime we would use crickets, and
on rare occasions, a spinning rod and reel. This was a far cry from
the offshore fantasy fishing world of Old Ahab. But the ditches
around the rice fields at Limerick, and the Cooper River itself,

teemed with such sporting delicacies as bream, bass, crappie, shell crackers and a few other very fine freshwater species. They were fun to catch and even more fun to have for supper. So, whenever possible, I headed for the rice fields for an afternoon of angling.

A Compleat Angler I was not. As hard as it was to admit, Courtenay was a far better fisherman than I—or Richard or Diji or Old Dad, the King! She had made a study of it, as she did most things, whereas I liked to catch whatever happened to let me catch it, though I did prefer giant largemouth bass. But Courtenay had a natural talent. She knew just when to go, where to stand on the bank, and with what bait, so that, more often than not, she would return from one of our expeditions with a sizable string of fish. More often than not, I was standing right beside her, with no results at all, while she pulled them in one after another. The boys wouldn't fish with her at all, which only went to show that the formidable male ego asserted itself early. She was not yet 10 and they were jealous!

Once, quite by accident, I did catch an enormous bass. I thought I had used great skill, if not aplomb, in landing this monster. When I'd had hardly a second to glory in my catch, a little nine-year-old boy who was visiting took one look at my fish and announced to the world that my bass was the very one he had caught the week before! (Shades of the duck blind!) "See the hole in his mouth?" he beamed, insinuating that the only reason I had been able to catch this fish was that he had so weakened it the week before. Someone was always trying to steal my trophies. Phooey on all nine-year-olds, including Courtenay!

When I first started coming to Limerick (before marriage), I was invited to go fishing in the Cooper River with Old Fiancé and his father, Old Bwana. I was thrilled. Not only would I have a chance to catch fish, but I would get to see this lovely tidal river from a superior vantage point—from the johnboat, in the river.

Prime fishing spots in those days were at the breaks in the banks of the old rice fields at the change of tides. A break was where an old bank had eroded away, and the tides could rush in and out unhindered. When the tide was going out, the water gushed with gusto, and the bass and bream boiled out with the water. It was exciting to watch. Alas, I was allowed to go, but not to fish.

Old Fiancé was at one end of the boat, Old Bwana at the other end, and I was consigned to the seat in the middle. That place in the middle of the boat was the pass-the-worms place! All I was allowed to do was to pass fore and aft while they reeled in the fish. Oh, well. I got to go in the river, and I had a good time in spite of my inferior rank.

It also gave me time to consider the comparison of this river and other rivers I had known. I still have a hard time saying "river" when talking about the waterways down here in the Lowcountry. After all, I grew up on the Ohio River. Now that was a river! First of all, the sheer beauty of the Cooper River, with its water an inky black, caused by the tannic acid from the roots of the cypress trees, was completely captivating in its pristine natural state. I also found it ever so awesome to see the endless miles of cypress planks that were used so long ago to shore up the banks of the rice fields and keep them from eroding. There, on the river, one could really appreciate the backbreaking labor it took to create the rice fields in the first place. It is said that it took ten years of construction before a plantation was ready for rice production. Many old docks along the river remained from the rice days, when barrels upon barrels of rice were loaded and sent to the port of Charleston, where they were milled and then shipped around the world.

Through the years, I came to know that there was a summer look to our rivers and a winter look, so different from each other that it was hard to recognize where you were in the river from one season to the next. The winter view is crisp, clear, and clean.

One can see clearly along the edges of the banks and into the rice fields and even to the plantation houses beyond. In the summer all this is obscured by dense foliage, quite like a jungle, so that seeing inward from the river is nigh impossible. The river itself is filled with vegetation, pigweed, duckweed, sometimes water hyacinths that clog the banks and disguise the entrances to the smaller creeks. It is lush and dark in its greenness.

This same dense verdure also entangled fishing hooks and hid the very fish one would like to catch. When I graduated from the pass-the-worms position, I sometimes would go fishing by myself in the river, and many a time I have had to cut my line in chagrin and disappointment, leaving it hanging in the weeds while I went home empty-handed. Oh woe, embarrassed, bitter woe.

One year, I was given a Mitchell 300 spinning reel and a rod for my birthday, and I enjoyed it as long as I could. My hook, line and sinker enjoyed a rather solid series of misadventures in every tree limb, root, stump or blackberry bush on the edges of every pond. Backlash was my middle name! I think the blackberries were my cruelest enemies. I waged a continuing battle against them with my new rod, and invariably, the bushes won. Of course, I would catch a few every now and then, just enough to keep my interest alive. Often, I thought to compare the lure of angling with that of a slot machine! The next cast just had to be the right one.

Though I have digressed in my ode to the river, I did love to fish, and I would sneak off to the river or the rice canals, leaving housewifely chores behind, just as often as I thought I could get away with it. One such day I remember with mixed emotions.

To go fishing on that day seemed just the right thing to do. I was really intent on catching dinner. Everyone was gone and I had the whole of Limerick to myself. I was alone! It was an idyllic day, birds singing, butterflies everywhere, the kind of day that made a person forget any problems or duties.

Consequently, I picked up my cane pole and cricket box and strode purposefully down the hill to the rice fields. "Today, I will tackle the Blackberry Corner," I mused with great resolve. This particular corner of the Boys' Pond was reputed to be one of the best fishing holes in all our ponds, if one could overcome the blackberry hedge that surrounded it. The water was deeper there, and I had been assured that the fish were a lot bigger as well. Also, in this place, the blackberry canes (and thorns) were more profuse, so one really had to be primed psychologically to even attempt the Blackberry Corner. Alone, and unfettered by guilt, I announced to the world that I was ready for this challenge.

It was possible, I found, to cast into the water at The Corner, but if a fish latched on, there was precious little I could do about it because my range of movement was so limited. By carefully balancing on an old barbed-wire fence (a false move here could send you to the fate suffered by Tar Baby), I could get my hook into the water. Then, by getting on all fours to peer through a hole in the thick bushes, I could see my cork. This was important. There were plenty of bites, but I missed every one. I had slipped into the slot-machine mode and just knew that the next bite would bring me three plums!

Thus, I tried and tried again where at first I had not succeeded. I was about to go crazy over losing so many crickets. Actually, it was not so much the crickets as it was what was eating them off my hook! Those fish had to be the size of whales! I knew, as sure as I was standing there, that this was the day I would catch the Granddaddy of all largemouth bass right there in the Blackberry Corner. I would be the champion of Limerick, because everyone in my household had been after the elusive Big One there—all unsuccessfully, I might add. It was important, therefore, that I figure a way to get at these tantalizing tormentors in that fishing hole of all fishing holes.

The sky was so blue, the air so fresh, everything so beautiful and peaceful. It seemed as though only God's creatures and I were left on this earth. What a glorious feeling! Without a single reminder of the outside world, I felt I hadn't a care in the world out there alone on the rice bank. But I did have a care in the world! I wanted that great big fish! Suddenly, like a lightning bolt out of the blue, a solution to this problem came to me, right out of that clear, blue sky! If, indeed, I was the only person in the world, why couldn't I just go out into the water and get that fish and forget the blackberries? No reason whatsoever. So I did what had never seemed so obvious before. I took off my slacks, hung them on a tree limb and waded right out to the edge of the Blackberry Corner to what I was positive would be an absolute triumph in the annals of bass fishing. There were no branches, no briars or intervening hindrances anywhere. I dismissed any thought of the other things that were in that pond with me. There is something to being single-minded.

The water was cool and I felt confident. Yet there in the middle of the water, cricket after cricket still kept disappearing down the gullet of what had to be the most enormous and elusive fish in history. It briefly crossed my mind that if I was not going to catch this monster, it would have been easier to blame the blackberries, and thus salve my ego. But as one cast led to another, I was happy and completely absorbed in the task at hand. Limerick was my wonderful world, and I was alone in it!

Imagine my dismay when I heard voices, many voices, on the bank, which completely destroyed my state of complete fish-absorption. It was also now quite obvious that I was no longer alone! I was not the only one in the world after all, and certainly not the only one who wanted to go fishing on this beautiful day. Elijah, our gentleman friend of color, and his entire family had decided too that this was an ideal day to fish, and they waved to me

as they piled out of the truck with buckets, poles and noisy good
cheer. It took me several minutes to realize in what a predicament
I found myself. I was in the middle of a twenty-acre pond, up
to my waist in water, and my pants were hanging on a branch,
acres away. Furthermore, I was surrounded by people! No cover
anywhere. Addressing this dilemma, I tried to sink deeper into the
water while I waved to them cheerily. Maybe they wouldn't notice.
I shouted that the fishing was really lousy in this pond, and perhaps
they would like to try the next pond over. Liar! Self-preservation
guided me, I suppose. No one should find the wife of the Earl of
Limerick pantless in the middle of a pond in the middle of the
day. Positively unseemly! I sank lower in the water as I pictured my
mother and mother-in-law clucking their tongues in dismay.
Taking me at my word (or just being tactful), the other fishermen
moved their buckets to the next pond, eagerly jabbering to one
another along the way. As soon as I thought it was safe enough,
I eased myself toward the bank, where I literally jumped into my
clothes! Gone was my feeling of being completely alone in the
world. Gone were my hopes of catching the biggest fish in the
Blackberry Corner. Gone were most of my crickets. Oh, well, I
thought, as I slogged up the hill with my empty bucket.
There would always be another day. And we would have pork
chops for supper.

Hoozit

I feel I must now talk about Hoozit, our second rabbit. When I think about Hoozit, the story that comes to mind also involves True Confessions from me, the storyteller. I hesitate to elaborate on this, but since it occupied so much of my time, I would be remiss if it were to be omitted from this literary effort.

I cannot remember how we happened to acquire Hoozit, the successor to Peter Rabbit, or even how he came to be named Hoozit, but to our house he did come, and within days he had established himself as even more of a character rabbit than was Peter. He was white, and he was large. True to Limerick form, Hoozit hated his pen, so he roamed free, thoroughly enjoying life on the old plantation. But Hoozit proved to be definitely peculiar in his own way.

While Peter Rabbit had loved the cat, Hoozit seemed to have inordinate affection for the cows! We had many cows, and Hoozit just loved them to death . . . all equally. While the cows munched away, Hoozit would bound out to meet them, a smile on his face as he ran little circles around each cow's nose. The cows didn't seem to mind, giving him a good sniff and then returning to their munching. Especially at night, he would hop on out into the middle of the herd, and then whatever kind of communication they may have had took place. We would watch Hoozit hop out, stand on his hind legs and lovingly pat a cow on her cheek. Yes, most unusual was this rabbit with the odd name of Hoozit!

All this is background for my true confessions. My interest in cows had a secret side to it that heretofore I have kept hidden. Having been raised in a home that was extremely Victorian, I was shielded from most worldly things. For instance, when I was a little girl, a bull was referred to as "a male cow"! Surely no household could utter the word "bull" out loud! When our own cow was sent away each year for artificial insemination, I had no idea what that meant, and it certainly was never explained to me. I am quite sure that my grandmother never imagined that such a sheltered life could lead to what it did for me. I am equally sure that it was the deprivation of worldly knowledge that led to my being extremely (and secretly) awed by the behavior of our elegant bull, Percy, towards our cows. In other words, I found myself completely engrossed in cow sex. There, you have it. My secret is out.

I have been known to skulk behind trees just to watch the flirtations of Percy and his harem, and I must admit that at times, his attentions were delivered with such ardor that I could scarcely believe my eyes. I experienced the same fascination with the lions at the zoo one time when they appeared to be in an obviously amorous mood, but wherever I was, at the zoo or behind a tree at Limerick, I never saw the accomplished fact. Something, or someone, always got in the way. Once, I saw Percy get mighty close. His future wife was drinking water from the pond, and I gather it was her turn to be in Percy's favor. Her position while drinking was utterly compromising, leaving her completely vulnerable from the rear. Percy took full advantage of the situation and set out to ravish her. I was behind my tree, silently clapping my hands in rapt anticipation, but alas, Percy over-assessed things and he sent the poor cow sprawling headfirst into the pond, never knowing what hit her . . . or perhaps she did. Hardly the most debonair way of wooing, I thought. He failed that time, but if there ever was a persistent Romeo, it was Percy, the Charolais bull!

I was just as persistent in my spying, but thousands of obstructions were thrown my way. The most frequent barrier was the fact that I felt I must hide my spying. Invariably, when the temptation to study life's ways presented itself, up would pop one of the children. I never was able to find a reasonable way to explain to them, or to anyone for that matter, that I had cow-sex on the brain. So I was furtive to the extreme and completely unsuccessful in my studies.

One afternoon, I thought I had it made . . . or Percy did, at least. From my studies, I had observed that if Percy was interested, so were many in his flock, especially those young "male cows." On this particular afternoon, it was blustery outside and I was sick in bed. It was my good fortune that our bedroom had glass on three sides so the room was ideal for viewing all sorts of things. While lying abed this day, I heard a noise outside and looked up to see a small herd of frenzied cows run by my window, with five young bulls in pursuit. Aha! I thought, and rose to rapt attention, completely forgetting that I was ailing. One poor cow in the group was the object of this amorous interest, and she was not at all sure she wanted anything to do with what was about to happen. She obviously had a "headache," so she led them a merry chase. As they lumbered around the corner again and again, worldly Percy exerted no undue energy in the chase. He just tagged along while the youngsters felt their oats and wore down their "victim."

"Neat!" I thought excitedly from my new position on the couch in my room. This vantage point certainly surpassed hiding behind trees. And no one was home except little old me!

By now, the chase had moved to the other side of the house, right outside the boys' room window, so it behooved me to change stations. Now they were mere feet from my nose, which was pasted against the glass, my body wrapped in the curtains. Finally, I was about to witness that which had been so elusive to me through the years. Surely, I was going to see IT!

Percy was now beginning to make his move but was having trouble with his young competition. They would not get out of his way. It was comical to see him getting more and more frustrated with these young bulls, and the cow, his "affianced," getting more and more "ready" . . . I guess "fatigued" is a better word. Percy would butt one little bull one way and another in the opposite direction. Sometimes he kicked at the tagalongs with great annoyance. There was no doubt about who was the boss in the Limerick world of cattle. And it certainly was clear who led the pack in the Love Category. Finally, positively asserting himself, Percy uttered one enormous bellow, followed with a snort, sending all and sundry interferences scattering in all directions. Now was his chance. Mine, too. I held my breath. Percy rolled his eyes significantly. Yes, IT was imminent, I felt sure.

The cow stood still and looked back at Percy with an "OK, if you must" expression, and Percy raised his nose in the air and uttered a very strange sound. This was it!

But, then . . . Shazam! Out jumped Hoozit the Super Rabbit, who landed with one big hop right at Percy's flaring nose. He should have had a cape! All he wanted to do was give Percy a pat on the cheek. Percy wore an expression of total disbelief and utter disgust. "Not now, you little creep," was the all-too-clear message. Who could blame him? With one huge snorting sneeze, he blew Hoozit head over heels out of his way. The rabbit tumbled down the hill.

Curses, foiled again! The cow caper was over. I returned to my sickbed. Poor Hoozit picked himself up and hopped off to contemplate what had just happened. Percy and the cow, now completely out of the mood, went out the gate together to munch lunch some more.

With that momentous un-happening, I gave up the idea entirely, nevermore to skulk behind a tree . . never, ever to see IT, or even care. Life was just too short. But Hoozit never gave up in his quest for friendship with an entire herd of cattle. What a rabbit!

The Pump

As the years at Limerick moved along, an interesting change in our duck world came to pass. It was duly noted by Old Ornithologist that the flyway for the ducks was moving, and that the type of duck coming to Limerick was different from what it had been in the past. Though the wood ducks (called summer ducks here) stayed all year, slowly but surely the mallards were being replaced by ducks who preferred deeper water. And that presented a snag in The Hunting Buddies' projection of a bigger, better duck season. Rice fields, by design, are not very deep, and our Big Field, being higher than the river, did not have the amount of water needed to be as attractive to the waterfowl as Old Blunderbuss would have liked. If he did not find a remedy for this problem, then the fine hunting at Limerick could be compromised. Months of research, and serious talks to The Hunting Buddies and Cronies at the Back Bar at The Club, led to a solution. I will agree that the resolution of the problem at hand far surpassed the idea of blowing holes in the rice fields with dynamite, but this solution was to become another bane of my existence. It came in the guise of The Pump.

I've always had a firm belief, further confirmed by experience, that man cannot fool Mother Nature. Although great things have been done towards tricking Mother Nature, I believe she always gets the upper hand. But St. Nick vowed he was not out to trick, only to help, Mother Nature. So The Pump was brought to The Patio for close study.

Unlike the rest of our so-called equipment, The Pump was brand-new, and it was bought for the express purpose of putting more water in the fields as was needed. I must say that for such an important piece of equipment, it was not particularly impressive in its appearance. It resembled a boat trailer, some 12 feet long, and in fact could be towed behind a car or tractor just as a trailer could be pulled. I was told that it had been developed for use in Vietnam for raising water from lower rice paddies to rice paddies on higher terraces. Since that was its exact mission here, The Pump was a sensible acquisition if we were to have a better duck season.

I am clueless as to just how it worked, but suffice it to say that it could be attached to the power take-out (PTO) of our trusty Ford tractor, which would then empower The Pump to suck water from the river and transfer it into the duck field through a long pipe, which was not unlike a huge vacuum-cleaner hose. This hose was about 12 to 14 inches in diameter. The process seemed simple enough. Stick one end of the hose in the river and one in the rice field, turn on the tractor, and *voilà*! You could pump the river dry and fill the pond as much as you wanted, all at the same time. Of course, there was much more to it than this. Just how this intricate machine could perform for us was to become an integral part of our daily lives at Limerick.

The Pump arrived in the summer. Our introduction to its capabilities came when The Saint decided to test it out by pumping the fishpond dry! "The fishpond" was the name given to our smallest rice field, the field nearest to the house. It was the only field that remained flooded year-round, and it was fed by a flowing artesian well that gushed water into it all the time. It was water from this well that fed all the rice fields when they were first filled. And it was this well that had been our salvation many a time when electric power was lost in Hell Hole Swamp and our other pumps were of no use to us. I have been Molly Pitcher at this well on too many occasions!

I thought it seemed at cross-purposes to drain a pond that had a steady source of water flowing into it, but how else could one learn the intricacies of the new pump? We teased Old Pumper that what he really wanted to do was to count his fish!

This operation took place on one beautiful weekend. The tractor was filled with fuel and placed at the edge of the pond. The Pump was attached and the hose let into the pond. The well was capped so no more water could enter. We were ready. We had an enlarged viewing party for this occasion, and we stood expectantly on the banks, watching with awe and admiration, as though we were attending a fine dramatic production. The tractor was started, and va-va-vroom! The hose sprang to life. It reminded me of a giant python stretched across the bank. As it filled with water, this great, fat hose bumped and jumped as though it were alive—and sick, because it soon spewed out its dinner at our feet! Courtenay liked to sit on the hose and have it bounce her around.

By mechanical magic, the pond was slowly emptied of its water, its fish, its frogs and its snakes. They all came pouring through the hose. The boys and friends were busy catching the flopping fish and putting them into buckets. Eventually, as the pond became nearly dry, only pockets of water were left in the deeper holes. The children then leaped into these holes and wrestled the larger fish into submission. It was quite a sight. Covered with mud, slipping and falling and shrieking with excitement, they waded into the holes that were churning with fish that were gasping, their mouths jutting upward like so many fish kisses. The boys said the large fish could butt them with the force of a goat. Still, they would grab one and pull it toward them, holding it in a tight bearhug to keep it from flipping away. It was a real rodeo, with whooping and hollering and cheers. I surmised that this might be the only time I would ever see a fish the size of my elusive Granddaddy Bass.

At the end of the day, the well was uncapped, the pond was refilled and many buckets of fish were returned to their home, more determined than ever to avoid our hooks, lines and sinkers in the future. As one of our friends loved to say, "Oh, well, another ho-hum day at Limerick."

The bottom line was that The Pump worked. I didn't have to think any more about The Pump for a couple of months—not, that is, until I received a frantic call from one of my friends in town whose son had taken part in our fish rodeo.

"Liz, you have to come over here right now! Your snake is loose in my house!" I could hear the consternation in her voice. And the tone was so accusatory!

"My snake?" I countered. "Whatever are you are talking about?"

I then was told how her son had secretly kept one of the snakes that had come through the pump hose on that fateful pond-pumping day. It was a small black racer, very shiny. He could beat his tail against the floor so fast it sounded very much like a rattlesnake, which didn't endear him to many in the human world. Richard's friend had sneaked this cute little varmint home and had kept it in the closet in his room on the top floor of their house, one of those tall, ancient, narrow houses of Charleston. I suppose Richard's buddy had snake tête-à-têtes when he wasn't at school, but on this day, the housekeeper had, by chance, bumped the box in the closet—and out came the snake and out went the housekeeper! General hysteria seized the household. Free at last, the little old snake slithered happily out the door into the sunny stair hall, where it inadvertently slipped over the edge of the stairs. He plummeted down all four stories, landing in the foyer, to the accompaniment of screams and slamming of doors. The stunned snake was then confined to one place and I was duly called. So now I am part of critter control, I thought as I drove towards town. I knew for sure that I was not going to get that snake, so I retrieved Richard from his school and he went in, smiled politely, and picked up the snake, and we then drove the 50 miles home with the snake in his lap. When we came to a stoplight, he would point the snake at the driver in the adjacent car and whoop with glee when he got the desired reaction. I was more than glad when we finally arrived home. Since he was now free from his shoebox, I can imagine the snake was glad, as well.

I promised earlier, as you might recall, that I would get back to the subject of drawbars on the tractor: For years, the borrowing of drawbars from Mepkin Abbey seemed a major part of my life.

Now that The Pump had been tried and proved worthy, it would soon be time to achieve proof of the pudding, so to speak. The last phases of preparation for duck season were at hand and the deepening of the big pond was nigh. The tractor and The Pump were moved to The Point and jockeyed into place. This was not easy, as the bank there is narrow and steep, without much room for maneuvering. Then the unspoken worries set in. Would The Pump pull the tractor backwards into the water? Would The Pump clog and break at low tide when it might suck up mud instead of water?

The tractor might run out of diesel fuel, and we had been warned that it must never run out of fuel. Did I say never? I meant never! Such an occurrence could be devastating to the tractor. I was warned that lines would then have to be blown out and motors taken apart before it would ever run again, so the better part of valor was to make sure it never ran out of fuel. Never.

With The Hunting Buddies on hand to kibitz, a 55-gallon drum was rigged on an elevated stand that would feed The Pump continuously, but that would need to be refilled periodically as well. Someone had to be responsible for this refueling, the greasing of the tractor and the checking up on it at all times. I was told that "It would take twenty-three days, twenty-four hours a day, to raise the water level."

So our lives became a twenty-three-day vigil—a vigil from hell! We all became that someone who looked after The Pump. I think I shall forever hear the drone of that tractor running all night and all day, in complete disharmony with the jangling jungle night sounds of Hell Hole Swamp, sounds that I had come to think quite beautiful. Diji and Richard did the bulk of the work, but I do remember one night when Elizabeth and I were the refueling appointees. We walked down towards the throbbing pump by the light of a silvery moon. Thank goodness for that moon (and a flashlight), because the banks could be pretty scary in the dark! But we persevered and did our job, as expected.

Those twenty-three days seemed to be a time of endless noise, taut nerves and short tempers, but the deed was accomplished and the discomfited feelings were replaced with self-satisfaction and the heady knowledge that all this tedious endeavor was bound to lead to a better duck season. The Big Pond was indeed fuller than it had been, and there was still water in the river. That was a relief! Duck Season was on the way to perfection! This, of course, was every good wife's goal in life.

That pump became an annual ordeal that was stoically endured by each of us, every October. I particularly dreaded this pump time because, invariably, when it came time to hook up The Pump, one part, the drawbar that hooked The Pump to the tractor, somehow, mysteriously, magically, malevolently, always disappeared.

Disappeared on its own, with no help from any of us. This is something like the misplaced shovel, the pliers and other tools, which always caused apoplexy for Old Pumper, battered eardrums for the youngsters, and work for me. The drawbar was the thing that enabled The Pump to stay attached to the tractor. In other words, it was essential to the exercise. So, more than once, I was sent up to Mepkin Abbey to borrow a drawbar from the monks. Besides being a monastery, Mepkin was a 3,000-acre working farm, so the monks had such tractor parts, and they knew where those were at all times. Also, they were very good neighbors, always glad to lend a hand—or drawbar—though many a time I was made to go to church before I was given the drawbar!

Through the years, we had become very good friends with the Abbey, and with Father Bernard, their business manager, in particular, because he had more access to the outside world. He was a frequent visitor at our house and a valued friend, and the donor of Arthur, Richard's best hen. He loved roast beef and enjoyed a Scotch whisky every now and then, which, I gather, was a rarity in monastic life. Also, he loved the opportunity to talk business with St. Nick. (It seemed quite nice to have both a saint and a Father at dinner!) They would stay up talking business until all hours of the night, and then Father Bernard would climb into his little green Beetle car and drive back home—often just in time for the first early morning prayer service.

Through Father Bernard and his community at Mepkin, I learned a great deal about the mysteries of monastic life and came to see the true spiritual importance of a contemplative order—far beyond the ignorant, clichéd beliefs of us worldly beings about monasticism. Forevermore, I shall be forever indebted to those cloistered men for their friendship, which went far deeper than lending me a drawbar!

One of the mornings that I was sent for the elusive drawbar

coincided with a special service at Mepkin: the anointing and blessing of the new church bell, named for Bernard of Clairvaux, the 10th-century founder of the Cistercian order in France. How fitting, I thought as I drove through the fog to Mepkin Abbey very early that morning. I had been invited to this service by Father Bernard, so there was a dual purpose to the visit: bells and drawbars!

Located on the west branch of the Cooper River, Mepkin is one of those unbelievably beautiful spots on earth. In the eighteenth century it became the rice plantation of Henry Laurens, one of South Carolina's most revered statesmen. In 1936, Mepkin and four adjacent plantations were bought by American icons Henry Luce and his wife, Claire Booth Luce. They wanted Mepkin as a winter home and hunting preserve. In 1949, Mrs. Luce donated the entire plantation to the Catholic Diocese of Charleston, which, in turn, established the abbey. It presented a perfect setting for the establishment of a Trappist monastery and has remained so ever since. The monks were wonderful neighbors to all who surrounded them.

The topography at Mepkin differs in the extreme from all other plantations, being a series of high bluffs with deep ravines between. The middle bluff, the highest bluff on the Cooper River, is a glorious spot, overlooking the old rice fields on both sides of the river. On a clear day one can see halfway to Charleston from this high bluff. It was on this forty-foot promontory that, in the 1760s, the historic Laurens house had been built. Sadly, it was lost long ago in a fire.

It was on the opposite bluff that the Luces built their house, and in time, a proper monastery was built on that site. The garden, commissioned in the 1930s of noted American landscape designer Loutrell Briggs, is filled with enormous azaleas and camellias. The ravine garden, planted with tropical water plants, is always a delight in its lushness. I often envied the monks their quiet heaven on earth. The echoes of the plantation's diverse past whispered through the grand trees at Mepkin, as the rice fields of another time intermingled with the serenity of the monastery.

So it was with pleasure that I arose very early to go to the special bell-anointing service that Sunday morning. The drawbar was secondary (for me).

As an outsider, one is a viewer rather than a participant in the monastery mass. After the Eucharist, we several guests followed the brothers out into the morning air and stood around the new bell tower with its large new bell atop. The fog hung thick on the bluff and the river below was barely discernible. Accompanied by two guitars, the singers' voices lifted straight to heaven. At the end of the hymn, a deep and resounding voice was heard from above and all eyes turned skyward. Was it God speaking? There, appearing high above us, was the abbot, who had climbed to the roof in order to reach the bell for the anointing and blessing. The traditional habit of this Trappist order consists of a white robe covered by a black surplice in the shape of a Latin cross. The sight of that black cross on the white, high above, with fog swirling around the abbot on high, was a riveting, powerful spiritual moment. I do believe that if I were ever to become a convert, this may have been the moment! As the Latin words of the benediction were intoned in deep, resonant cadences, as though on cue, a flight of six mallard ducks flew in perfect formation behind the abbot and then disappeared into the mist. I was so moved I nearly forgot the drawbar! I have jokingly said so on many occasions, but perhaps Hell Hole Swamp truly is heaven! Certainly, Mepkin Plantation is very close to it.

As time went on, I became well-known at Mepkin. My plantation tours took me there often, and I was often called by the abbot to give tours to visitors. The brothers referred to me as "the tour lady." Also, the once-a-year need for the drawbar made me a regular. We seemed quite at ease with our sacred and profane relationship that continues still.

On another October morning a couple of years later, the need for a drawbar was made vociferously clear, so I phoned the monastery and asked for Father Bernard. I was told he was outside and couldn't come to the phone, to which I countered, "Well, ask him not to leave. I need to come borrow a drawbar. I am leaving right now."

So, off I scurried, driving as quickly as I could the twelve miles that separated our two plantations, a route very familiar to me now. The last few miles meandered through endless pine forests, all part of the 3,000 acres owned and managed by the monks at Mepkin. I was just approaching this area when lo, I spotted Father Bernard's little green Beetle car, speeding off in the opposite direction.

"Oh, no!" I said to myself. "I told him not to leave until I got there." That is not how one should think when referring to a Father—a bit cheeky, one would say—but no Father Bernard, no drawbar. The tranquility of my family life was on the line here. So, I U-turned in the road and took up the chase after the green Beetle. I honked my horn and waved, to no avail. If anything, he went faster. I tried harder to catch up, honking the horn and waving, with no results. I was getting exasperated when the Beetle turned off the paved road onto a country lane. I followed as he twisted and turned through the pines for two or three more miles, maybe farther, with me waving and beeping my silly horn. Finally, the Beetle turned into a clearing where there was a small, very humble cabin. Shades of Hansel and Gretel, I thought as I turned in after him. At last I had caught up. I was about to leap out with a happy "haloo," when the Beetle door opened and out stepped—not Father Bernard, but another of the cloistered brethren. He was ashen-faced! Not only was he forbidden to talk except when absolutely necessary, but especially not to women. All he was trying to do was to deliver some eggs to a poor family when he found himself being chased down the road by a madwoman—and a loud one at that! His eyes showed his anxiety (terror might be a better word). I was mortified. Choking back my embarrassment, all I could stammer was, "Oh, I am so sorry . . . I thought you were Father Bernard." Of course, this only compounded the problem, as it made it sound as though I always chased Father Bernard through the forest. There was no righting this wrong, I decided, so I backed out and resumed my route to the monastery and the drawbar. My mission was ultimately accomplished, but I don't believe I shall ever forget the expression on that monk's face.

As long as Limerick was ours, we pumped the river all but dry each year. It is my understanding that The Pump is still in use and working just fine in another place. I wonder who the drawbar-fetcher is.

In the meantime, I continue my friendships at Mepkin Abbey, which is now a much more open community, welcoming people from across the country to its little piece of heaven on Hell Hole Swamp earth.

Lost

An ill wind was blowing toward Limerick, and we were caught in its maelstrom. As a result, I had an extraordinary experience, one that shall long remain in my memory. I got lost in the forest!

Limerick was not the only plantation on the Cooper River, nor was it anywhere near the largest, but it was one of the few on which real people lived all year long. No one lived on the plantation across the river from Limerick, but we knew it had recently been surveyed from stem to stern, and the rumor was that it was for sale. Combined with other recent rumors that a rail spur was to be built in our neighborhood (news that we could find precious little information about), our curiosity was aroused. No one was building railroads these days. Why here and why now? The rumors persisted, so, piqued by concern for our future, an adventurous spirit, and a well-known nosiness, I went to see for myself if I could discover just what was going on next door. This might have been considered trespassing, but when the gossip continued that this plantation

...hice, clearly flagged path, there were now dozens of survey lines. ...spokes on a wheel, they radiated in all directions. The orange ...s taunted me. I knew I was close to the river, and I knew that ...old dock was to my left somewhere, but I was also finding that ...survey lines led me nowhere. Imperceptibly, I began to realize ...I was not going to discover all I wanted to know that day, and ...I should retrace my steps and go home. After all, I had been ...king for several hours.

...Turning to go back across the wild turkey bridge, it was soon ...parent that I couldn't find it! Why, I was there just ten minutes ...fore! Scrambling back and forth with no success, it slowly ...wned on me that, at the very least, I had become completely ...rned around. It was quite possible that I was lost.

...As the shadows began to lengthen, I knew that I could not ...ford the luxury of a rest. The better part of valor was to follow the ...ver trail, since I knew the river would pass the old dock. There, I ...uld get my bearings, or even swim across to Limerick if I had to. ...rambling along, ducking vines and trying to avoid brambles, my ...et hurt and my back ached. I was also hungry and thirsty. Finally, ...t the end of a tunnel-like maze of underbrush, I came to a place ...here I could straighten up. Looking around, I found myself in a ...learing on the side of the hill, and there in front of me was, not ...gingerbread house, but the roofless ruin of a rather large brick ...building. Was it a mirage? I was spellbound. But then I knew: the ...ilk barn. It had to be the old silk barn. No one I knew had seen ...t for decades.

Silk had been manufactured in South Carolina in the earliest ...of days in the hope that it would become a lucrative crop for ...the new Carolina. In fact, the name of this plantation was Silk ...Hope! Two stories high, the remaining walls of the building were ...made of Carolina Gray brick, probably made right here on the ...Cooper River. They were covered with vines. The brick was laid

was due for alterations in the name of industrial progress, any legal worries about treading on others' soil were easily set aside. If indeed there was to be a railroad built in our own backyard, then I thought that perhaps I could follow the surveyors' flags and uncover the proposed, but secret, route of this rumored, nefarious train track. Thus it was that I found myself in the midst of a forest primeval, on one beautiful afternoon in Hell Hole Swamp.

What a gorgeous day it was to be out of doors! The Saint, not disagreeing that I might come across some clues, delivered me and trusty Bobo to the roadside near Quenby Creek, the site of a very important Revolutionary War skirmish. From there, it was my plan to follow the survey line, to what end I knew not. So there I was on this brilliant November day, with faithful Bobo, walking through land that had, for so long, remained untouched by the present world. Since the ruinous days following the Civil War, the land here had, bit by bit, reverted to its natural, wild state. The original house had long since crumbled, the rice banks had gone to ruin, and the rice fields were grown over with new forest. When I say "new," that is a relative term, because the pines that towered above me reached right up to the heavens. Enormous oaks spread wide and leafy over history-laden earth. There were signs of deer and other wild creatures everywhere, and the air jangled with the call of the pileated woodpecker. The river flowed deep and black between Limerick and this densely forested plantation.

I had no trouble following the path made by the surveyor's ax, marked with twirling orange tapes. Feeling once more a bit like Hansel or Gretel, I wondered if there might be a gingerbread house and a wicked witch somewhere ahead. I had heard legends of ancient buildings and the grave of the third Royal Governor of South Carolina, Sir Nathaniel Johnson, that were hidden somewhere in this jungle-like undergrowth, so why not a gingerbread cottage? The wicked witch in the present scenario was the mysterious railroad and where its route might eventually go.

The sun was high in the sky, and as it filtered through the trees, dappled patterns of light danced capriciously over the earth. This caused my mind to stray from Hansel and Gretel and wander to a distant college prom where a revolving mirrored ball had created just such an effect on a dance floor. With a fleeting thought about whatever happened to that distant beau, What's-his-name, I pulled my attention back to my mission.

The carpet of leaves crunched underfoot as I strode along, and the air was crisp and invigorating. The surveyor's path led purposefully deeper into the woods and away from the highway sounds. Soon, I was alone and detached from the worldly world. I felt amazingly humbled and unimportant in the total dominance of Nature. I had never seen such trees. Perhaps it was because of the natural phosphate that was found on these plantations in the last century, but there was no doubt in my mind that these pine trees were huge in comparison to any I had ever seen elsewhere. There was a fallen pine to my left, and I climbed up on it to see how long it was. I stepped off eighty-one paces! The trees that were upright were of equal height or more, and with the sunlight pouring through it, the forest seemed transformed into a towering Gothic cathedral. Drenched in its splendor, I continued to follow the survey line, which cut like a central aisle down the nave of my forest cathedral.

Then I came to the old logging road. Many times, The Saint and I had gone down this road to reach the river, so I knew it led from the highway to the river, perpendicular to my present direction. Down there at the river, remnants of the old rice planting days were in evidence everywhere, as were the signs of the timber days of the early part of the twentieth century, when this land was owned by a timbering company from North Carolina. The broken dikes were now covered with red cedars and wax myrtles and were very

probably populated with all sorts of serpents an end of that old road, the pilings of a once huge dock broke out of the water like bristles on a gr The length of that old dock bespoke the immen antebellum days. A newer dock with a ramp of r the timbering days on this river, when great rafts floated with the tides down to the harbor in Cha

My romantic side reeled at thoughts of those d had been there, but what were they like? What so on here? I would love to go back in time, just for a discover the answers to my many questions.

Still following the orange surveyors' tags, I cross road and plunged into the denseness once more. T downward, so I knew I was getting nearer to the riv and eroded, ancient dikes crisscrossed the terrain. T earthworks, left from the rice plantations, are to be f in nearly every woods along every river in lower Sou constant reminders of the vastness of the former rice

As the going got steeper and wetter, I was glad it w when, presumably, the snakes and alligators were asle an old canal at the bottom of the hill, and some tree r nice footbridge for me. But, at midcrossing, I was star death by a terrific clamor all around me. I nearly fell i I had disturbed six colossal wild turkeys that were now gobbling their way to the tip-tops of the pine trees. I h but one wild turkey in my life, and I certainly never dre could fly so high. In fact, I never knew that they could f Bobo was equally awestruck! We stood very still until th to their own special turkey place.

The path had now become much more difficult to foll thicker, wetter and rougher. I was stumbling a lot and wa beginning to feel the heat my activity generated. Also, ins

up in Flemish bond, and the segmental arches over the windows and doors, as well as the fireplace keystone, exemplified the sophisticated craftsmanship found in early eighteenth-century Carolina. The wooden doorsills were charred black from a fire that must have consumed the building. When? Forest fire? Lightning? War? Questions again. There were several steps leading from a central doorway, and I sat down on them. Bobo, also bone-weary, settled at my feet. I have always been utterly enthralled by any and all antique ruins, and here, hidden away in these tangled woods, I had found one of my own.

The sun was on its final descent and the whole world was vibrant with light. As I sat there on those old brick steps, every pine needle seemed ablaze, and the burnished copper color of the cypresses was brilliant. I was transfixed, mesmerized by the shimmering light. What was happening? Where was I? Who was I? I was No One. All was Beauty. The scene was an ethereal reality, but then, as suddenly as it had appeared, it was gone!

As the sun dropped from sight, I was jolted back to my senses. I remembered I was lost—well, not really lost, but I was having some difficulty rediscovering the way to being unlost! All I had to do was to find that old logging road before dark. I was so glad that Bobo was with me. Swimming seemed a bad idea, if not an outright stupid one.

Since the orange tapes were no good to me, I resolved to follow the glow in the western sky. I hurried. My boot would not stay tied. I tripped often on roots. Briars pulled at my clothes. Finally, I stumbled and fell into the mushy, murky marsh. My heart was pounding and I could feel panic welling up. I struggled up, and the night sounds seemed to crescendo to an excruciating decibel. The trees were silhouetted like grotesque giants. They had been so beautiful earlier in the day! A small limb clutched at my arm and I stifled a scream, sinking to the ground breathless and beaten.

My imagination had gone amok! The snakes were awake, there was quicksand in the next puddle, I could fall into a hidden well! Egad! I was going to cry! I hugged Bobo tight.

I smacked at a mosquito. I suppose that there is nothing in the word like a cloud of mosquitoes to snap a body back to reality! I remembered the phantom silk barn, and I couldn't wait to tell the family about it. That was all I needed to get going again. I got up, took a deep breath and plunged once more into the dimness.

No more than ten yards away, I stumbled out of the thicket and onto the logging road! The moon had risen, and it lit my way the entire three miles to the highway, where I found The Saint hallooing as he paced up and down the road. I do believe he was worried. It was 9 o'clock at night, and I was certainly glad to see him.

Now, safely back at home, everything was all right—or was it? It was obvious that there was a definite plan afoot that could unseat us here at Limerick. My enthusiasm for the mysterious brick building encouraged The Saint to go with me the next day to have a view for himself. We couldn't find it anywhere. It had to remain lost, as I had been the night before, Silk Hope's own mystery.

That magnificent heritage of priceless natural beauty at Silk Hope did, after all, have a price. Within months, it would be sold. Limerick would soon follow. Verily, a railroad would cut through all. The deer would be gone, the turkeys would go, and those splendid trees were in peril. All was to be lost. What was found?

The Last Thanksgiving

Our fears had been well-founded and the handwriting was on the wall. A new railroad would cut through Limerick like a knife, separating us from the river, crossing all the rice fields, cutting through the upper dove field. You'd be able to see it from every window in the house. We were powerless against the politics behind the railroad, our frustration was absolute and our Limerick was to slip away from us. Each one of us would soon be facing a new beginning. In no way could we retrieve the way our lives had been for these past years, nor should we try. No matter what might be our wishes, it was out of our hands. We had fought the best fight we knew how at unbeatable odds, and though it was heart-rending and life-altering, we were going to have to move on.

All the required environmental impact studies had been completed, even to recording the sounds of the night! A hurried archaeological dig had produced a grid of square pits, dug in what I thought were unlikely places to find anything. As expected, they didn't find anything of world-shaking importance. In fact, the bits and pieces that surfaced during my walks were more noteworthy!

However, some interesting things did come to light. For instance, the foundations of the original eighteenth-century Limerick house had been dug out, and it was intriguing to see the original basement floor laid with large, square pavers of Portland stone and a floor plan that coincided with written descriptions. Since this was all to be covered over by the railroad tracks, never to be seen by anyone ever again, Courtenay and I, by ourselves, dug out these stones, determined to move them with us when we ultimately had to leave.

I might add that having an archaeological dig on one's property, when the purpose was not wholly to discover the past but to speedily satisfy an impact study, was not entirely peaches and cream. We were literally invaded by an army of very young diggers, many not much older than our own children. In no time at all, the children became involved in the dig, and then it wasn't long before my pots and pans, along with most of our pillows, were usurped by the diggers who were squatting on our soil in their little tented compound. This was not a happy time, and I could see small scholarly gain from the energy and money spent on it.

Be that as it may, some legal boondoggles arose that precluded the finalizing of our departure, so we lived on at Limerick in a state of borrowed time. I remember a great-aunt of my father's who continually celebrated her last Christmas—for about nine years. Well, we didn't hang on quite that long, but suffice it to say that we had more than one last set of holidays while the legal pundits plodded on and the desecration of our beloved Limerick continued even though the legal transfer of Limerick was not finalized. I had a feeling that the railroad faction was not convinced that we didn't have a trump card yet to play that would halt the building of the railroad. We did not, but their paranoia became apparent on the

Thanksgiving Day I shall call our Last Thanksgiving. I should like to recount that day, because it will remain in the minds of all the family as something much more than just a poignant last supper.

For our family, Thanksgiving had always been the most fun holiday of the year at Limerick. The weather was always fine, the humidity of the summer months now long past, replaced by the crispness in the air usually invigorating but not quite freezing.

I have fond memories of my first Thanksgiving at Limerick, which occurred not very long after my arrival from Kentucky. As mentioned, I was new to the territory then, new to this family, and certainly new to the dynamics of feasting in Hell Hole Swamp. St. Nick's father was a carver par excellence, a time-honored symbol of Southern noblesse oblige. The feast involved not only wild turkey, but venison and duck as well, all needing to be carved. I had never tasted any of this wild game. Also, I had been used to cold, sometimes even snowy Thanksgivings in Kentucky, and there we were, out on The Patio where the dining table had been moved, so we could enjoy our Thanksgiving dinner alfresco on a glorious November afternoon. I was terribly impressed and felt as though I were part of some medieval monarchy, where bones could be (and were) tossed to the castle dogs.

Of course, not every Thanksgiving dinner was to be enjoyed out of doors, but there was always a veritable cornucopia of fine foods to be savored. Afterwards, there was all that space to play in, depending upon your generation. Limerick was good for that at all times, not just for special occasions, but on Thanksgiving, there was something wonderful about having those leafy spaces available to us. Walks could be made, naps could be taken, skeet could be shot, not to mention ending the day by creeping down to the wood duck pond to watch the ducks come in to roost and then returning to the house for the perfect turkey sandwich. No hunting was allowed on Thanksgiving Day at our house.

On this Last Thanksgiving, it was in everyone's heart that this was to be the biggest and the best of all, and we expected a rather large number of guests. Both boys were home from prep school and had brought friends with them. A lot of my family was coming, and we also were expecting Father Bernard, who had been such a stalwart friend through all our trying times. The Saint was coming from Myrtle Beach, where he had moved his business. We would be a goodly lot, and there would be a great deal of stirring the pot to get it all together. The house was full, filled with laughter, and we all were in good form. We were in agreement that this would be a celebration, not a funereal experience! That, at least, was our plan.

At about 5:30 in the morning on Thanksgiving Day, I was awakened by the roar of motors in the distance that grew louder and louder by the minute. I shook myself awake and ran to the door where I could see, rumbling through the avenue, several trucks and three giant bulldozers. They went crashing across the avenue, and each bulldozer had a spiked protrusion on its front, raised to midway height. They were fearful-looking weapons of destruction. Forgetting any modesty I may have felt otherwise, I flew out the door in my nightgown and raced towards the avenue. I met the foreman halfway and literally screamed at him: "What are you doing here today? It is Thanksgiving!" I must say he looked terribly embarrassed, even ashamed, but he explained he had been ordered to begin clearing the route for the railroad today. I burst into tears of frustration and boo-hooed all over him, his car, and my nightgown. After all the other things we had been made to face, I just couldn't think of a meaner ploy. I do believe they were so afraid that we would arouse the save-the-tree sorts that they thought they'd catch us off guard if they came at dawn on a holiday.

They were right. We were caught off guard, and right before my eyes, the first bulldozer rammed its spikes into one of the huge oak trees and continued to do so until it lay in an ignominious pile of

splinters and jagged tree parts. It was then unceremoniously
run over, as a tank would do on the field of battle, and the
bulldozer moved on to another tree. It was unbelievable. As they
slammed into the next tree, which was the largest and known as
The Limerick Oak, I stumbled back into the house and began to
stuff the turkey. I was numb with sadness and defeat. Our beautiful
Limerick was being destroyed right in front of our eyes. And it
was Thanksgiving!

By now, the entire household was awake and horrified and
incensed. The deafening noise of crackling trees breaking and
falling was with us all day as preparations for our last feast
continued. My mother was cooking her part of dinner at her little
house, which was much closer to the avenue than our house. (In
fact, eventually, it, too, went under the bulldozer.) Others, those
who were staying in The Bunk House, were also using that kitchen
with the goal of making our Last Supper a wonderful one. But no
matter how we tried to put on a brave front, there was a pall over
everything and everyone.

The day wore on and the other guests began to arrive, one
by one. Each gasped as he drove in the avenue and viewed the
destruction in progress. The Saint was ashen, and his clenched jaw
was obvious. How hard this was for him! Limerick had been his
greatest lifelong dream. I was glassy-eyed as the realization of the
true end of our days at Limerick loomed large.

Just as Father Bernard was coming down the avenue in his little
green Beetle, he was forced to slam on his brakes as a startling thing
occurred. It brought everyone and everything on the place to a halt.
No one could or would dare move. Everything seemed as though it
were in slow motion. Time stood still at 12:15 p.m. on this, our last
Thanksgiving at Limerick Plantation.

At that very moment, the hated bulldozer driver (only doing
what he was told, mind you) rammed, full force, I assume

inadvertently, into the electric light pole, bringing it crashing down on top of him, swathing him in electric wires. A loud explosion and great puff of smoke followed. Would we be having fried bulldozer driver for dinner instead of turkey? What an awful thing to think, but it did cross my mind. If it crossed anybody's mind, it was the mind of that driver, who undoubtedly thought his time to meet his maker had come. He sat stone-still, wrapped in coils of wire, afraid to make any move at all for fear of electrocution. Though covered with soot, he was miraculously unharmed. No live wires, just a mess, and no electric power. Father Bernard leaped from his car to go to the man's aid. We hadn't thought of that!

At the very moment of impact, explosion and poof of smoke, my mother was driving over to our house with the squash pie and cranberry mold, her Thanksgiving specialties, carefully placed on the front seat of her car. She was nearly beside the bulldozer when the accident took place, and it so shocked her (pun) that she drove directly into one of the archaeological pits, headfirst! So while the man on the bulldozer literally shook in his boots, her car was perched at a dizzying cant. You can imagine the condition of the cranberry mold as it plopped all over the squash pie and the front seat of the car. I wasn't close enough to hear what she said as she climbed from that pit! It was just as well. Poor Father Bernard was hard pressed to know which way to turn.

It was an untoward way to slow things down, but quiet reigned at Limerick at last! The bulldozer was silenced, and the driver, very thankful not to be dead, went home to his own Thanksgiving dinner. All motors were off, as there was no electricity. Fortunately, the turkey was nearly done and we could finish the rest of the food on the gas stove in the bunkhouse. We set up a big trestle table on The Patio, pulled out all the good silver, and the girls made a stunning centerpiece of fall leaves and pumpkins.

We took lots of pictures and acted silly. And we gave thanks.

We were thankful to be together. We were thankful that there were no deaths that day. We were especially thankful for all those unbelievably wonderful years that our family had, and for the love we all had for this bit of land—a precious place like Limerick, which we had been lucky enough to call home. For this we should be eternally grateful, because in our hearts, no matter where we might go, Limerick would always be home. It was "meet and right" to be thankful.

Because of the legal shenanigans, this turned out not to be our last Thanksgiving at Limerick, and the stay of execution afforded us one more holiday feast in Hell Hole Swamp before we each embarked on our next adventures.

From our profound sadness, what we eventually came to appreciate was the priceless knowledge that what had been our very special, and much-loved, home was made even more precious by its loss. The memories of that wonderfully alive period in our lives can never be lost—nor can they be revived. But life would be good again—somewhere—for indeed, home is in the heart.